Cambridge Elements ≡

Elements in Bioethics and Neuroethics
edited by
Thomasine Kushner
California Pacific Medical Center, San Francisco

ROLES OF JUSTICE
IN BIOETHICS

Matti Häyry
Aalto University School of Business

CAMBRIDGE
UNIVERSITY PRESS

CAMBRIDGE
UNIVERSITY PRESS

University Printing House, Cambridge CB2 8BS, United Kingdom

One Liberty Plaza, 20th Floor, New York, NY 10006, USA

477 Williamstown Road, Port Melbourne, VIC 3207, Australia

314–321, 3rd Floor, Plot 3, Splendor Forum, Jasola District Centre,
New Delhi – 110025, India

103 Penang Road, #05–06/07, Visioncrest Commercial, Singapore 238467

Cambridge University Press is part of the University of Cambridge.

It furthers the University's mission by disseminating knowledge in the pursuit of
education, learning, and research at the highest international levels of excellence.

www.cambridge.org
Information on this title: www.cambridge.org/9781009108478
DOI: 10.1017/9781009104364

First published 2022

A catalogue record for this publication is available from the British Library.

ISBN 978-1-009-10847-8 Paperback
ISSN 2752-3934 (online)
ISSN 2752-3926 (print)

Cambridge University Press has no responsibility for the persistence or accuracy of
URLs for external or third-party internet websites referred to in this publication
and does not guarantee that any content on such websites is, or will remain,
accurate or appropriate.

Every effort has been made in preparing this Element to provide accurate and up-to-date
information which is in accord with accepted standards and practice at the time of
publication. Although case histories are drawn from actual cases, every effort has been made
to disguise the identities of the individuals involved. Nevertheless, the authors, editors, and
publishers can make no warranties that the information contained herein is totally free from
error, not least because clinical standards are constantly changing through research and
regulation. The authors, editors, and publishers therefore disclaim all liability for direct or
consequential damages resulting from the use of material contained in this Element. Readers
are strongly advised to pay careful attention to information provided by the manufacturer of
any drugs or equipment that they plan to use.

Roles of Justice in Bioethics

Elements in Bioethics and Neuroethics

DOI: 10.1017/9781009104364

First published online: July 2022

Matti Häyry

Aalto University School of Business

Author for correspondence: Matti Häyry, matti.hayry@aalto.fi

Abstract: This Element traces the origins and development of bioethics, the principles and values involved in the discipline, and the roles of justice among these principles and values. The main tasks given to the concept of justice have since the late 1970s been nondiscrimination in research, prioritization in medical practice, and redistribution in healthcare. The Element argues that in a world challenged by planet-wide political and environmental threats this is not sufficient. The nature and meaning of justice have to be rethought. The Element does this by dissecting current bioethical approaches in the light of theories of justice as partly clashing interpretations of equality. The overall findings are twofold. Seen against the background of global concerns, justice in bioethics has become a silent guardian of economic sustainability. Seen against the same background, we should set our aims higher. Justice can, and must, be put to better use than it currently is. This title is also available as Open Access on Cambridge Core.

This Element also has a video abstract:
www.cambridge.org/rolesofjusticeinbioethics

Keywords: bioethics, justice, equality, principles, social, ecological

ISBNs: 9781009108478 (PB), 9781009104364 (OC)

ISSNs: 2752-3934 (online), 2752-3926 (print)

Contents

1 Two Theses and the Order of Things

- The role of justice in bioethics is to perpetuate capitalist hegemony.
- The role of justice in bioethics should be to reclaim moral and political concepts for resistance and emancipation.

These are the two theses that I present and defend in this treatise.

They may sound like battle cries, but they are statements of fact. By capitalist hegemony I mean the belief that perpetual material growth is necessary and inevitable. By resistance I mean opposition to this belief, and by emancipation the state of not being in its grip anymore. I will clarify these further during the course of my inquiry.

The first thesis is descriptive, and its defense comprises historical and rational reconstructions of bioethics, justice in bioethics, and the way considerations of justice in bioethics lend support to the agenda of unceasing material growth. The analysis contains no explicit value judgments.

The claim is quite general, though. Some bioethicists are sure to point out that their work does not further the capitalist agenda, and they may be right. I will try to show that in many cases appearances are deceptive. The work of bioethicists can have an indirect impact that they do not anticipate. When I encounter cases where my assertion becomes untenable, I will heed and make a note of the limits of my argument.

The second thesis is conditionally prescriptive. Its defense requires a critique of never-ending material growth, explications of resistance and emancipation as alternatives to it, and an interpretation of justice-related concepts in bioethics that allows them to support resistance and emancipation.

I will begin by describing bioethics as a practice (Section 2) and as an academic discipline (Section 3). I will then go on to describe two distinct takes on justice in academic bioethics (Section 4) and show, by using a map of justice as competing interpretations of equality, how considerations based on them either indirectly support the idea of everlasting growth or create distractions that hamper its critical analysis (Section 5). These will form the bulk of my defense of the first thesis.

I will then examine two contenders for justice beyond capitalism in bioethics, namely social justice and global justice. While they provide important criticisms against the excesses and failures of the system, they do not question it on a deeper level. I identify the business-as-usual approach as the worst culprit and argue that even social and global justice do not challenge it adequately (Section 6). This will complete my defense of the first thesis and form the core of my defense of the second one.

After an illustrative detour to continuous growth, conservation, sustainability, and sustainable development (Section 7), I will demonstrate (Section 8) how theories of justice can form coalitions that explain the failure to proceed toward emancipation and liberation. These will include alliances between libertarianism, communitarianism and the rights and capabilities approach, utilitarianism and communitarianism, and care ethics and the rights and capabilities theory.

I will conclude by suggesting (Section 9) that collaboration between two currently antagonistic approaches to moral and political thinking could provide a route to emancipation. If care ethicists and utilitarians could bury their hatchets, they could, I argue, offer solid resistance against the views that support the current hegemony. This collaboration is unlikely because the theoretical presuppositions of the doctrines are wide apart, but I will give an outline of how it could be developed.

2 Bioethics as a Practice Arising from Other Practices

2.1 Early Medicine, Healthcare, and Medical Research

The practice of bioethics developed historically in parallel with the practices of medicine, healthcare, and medical and biological research. The early organization of medical research and training in Mesopotamia, Egypt, India, China, Greece, and Rome gave rise to ethical instructions to physicians, preserved for posterity in the Hippocratic oath.[1] The art and its etiquette were continued and passed on during the Middle Ages by Byzantine[2] and Islamic[3] medicine, while healthcare provision in Catholic Europe was mostly reduced to nursing and traditional healing in monasteries. Although during the Renaissance universities and their medical schools were established and research increased also in Catholic European cities, the age-honored paradigm of humoralism, or theory of body fluid balance, did not allow any quantum leaps in medical knowledge or practice. Surgery without anesthesia was crude, letting blood was a common solution to ailments, and apart from opium, quinine, and folk remedies medication consisted mainly of poisonous metal-based compounds.[4]

Some elements of medical and nursing ethics emerge quite naturally from these practices. The starting point is the principle of beneficence. People seeking the advice and help of healers assumed and expected some good to come out of it, and the Hippocratic oath confirmed the physician's commitment to this by stating, among other things: "Into whatsoever houses I enter, I will enter to help the sick." The principle of nonmaleficence, or "Do no harm," complemented and balanced the idea of doing good in the Oath. Later on, possibly in the seventeenth century, the prohibition was made paramount by the Latin phrase "Primum non nocere" – "First of all, do no harm."

This emphasis seems eminently reasonable in a time of hazardous surgery, induced bleeding, and toxic drugs.

In addition to these two rules for physicians, the care work undertaken by nuns in monasteries had links to the principles of vulnerability and dignity. The women, often from affluent families who financed the monasteries, performed their Christian duty by responding to the otherwise unmet needs of the vulnerable poor, and the suffering of the poor was seen as the cornerstone of their dignity and the route to their salvation. These ideas will make a comeback in this narrative at a later stage, in a clarification of the different foundations of welfare states and public health programs.

The professional status of physicians and other caregivers was clarified when first Spain and then other European powers started licensing medical practitioners in the sixteenth and seventeenth centuries.[5] This regulative practice of bioethics and biolaw was, no doubt, needed as the healthcare market was dominated by self-taught barber-surgeons, midwives, apothecaries, drug peddlers, and other snake-oil sellers. It is, however, also an early example of medical doctors asserting their influence to achieve a monopoly in their field. This will have a bearing when the story has proceeded to the nineteenth-century anti-abortion campaign in the United States.

Surgeons were for long a caste of their own, separate from medical doctors. Although anatomy and surgery were taught in the new universities of Bologna, Padua, and others, the division of labor remained, echoing the prohibition of "using the knife" in the Hippocratic oath. Two ethical rules and principles are directly linked with the activities of surgeons. Research in the field was hampered by a ban on dissecting cadavers, which was lifted only sporadically and for relatively short periods of time before the dawn of modern medicine.[6] Dignity in some sense plays a role in the longevity of this taboo. In a more forward-looking vein, amputations without sedation or effective painkillers turned out to be more successful with the patient's consent. This had little or nothing to do with autonomy and self-rule as we now know them – it was more a question of compliance providing convenience – but it is a terminological landmark in the prehistory of bioethics all the same.[7]

Urbanization, wars, poor sanitation, and colonialism boosted the spread of contagious diseases, and pandemics decimated populations all over Europe and wiped out or lethally maimed entire Indigenous communities and nations elsewhere. Humoral medicine could not cope with these diseases, but as contact had been identified as a partial culprit, the spread of plague and other pestilences was contested by isolation periods for ships entering harbors. The length of the isolation was set to forty days by a fifteenth-century Venetian ruling, and quarantine (in Italian, "quaranta" means forty) was born, although similar distancing measures had been in use much earlier in other cultures.[8]

Contagious-disease control marked the recovery of European public health policy, which had gone into decay for a millennium after the downfall of the Western Roman Empire. Physicians were again trained, albeit in inadequate numbers and, partly because of a shortage of cadavers for dissection, mostly by books and lectures. With the Reformation, Catholic monasteries were closed in Protestant countries, but secular dispensaries for the poor started to replace them in the eighteenth century.[9] Insofar as their motivation was to meet the needs of the worst off, they, together with the monasteries, formed the foundation of socialized medicine in the continent and gave budding embodiments to public solidarity and social justice.

A pivotal example of practice, functional and dysfunctional, giving rise to ethical and jurisprudential thought and codification is Thomas Percival's 1803 book *Medical Ethics*.[10] In 1789, the city of Manchester in England experienced a serious epidemic of typhoid fever, and Percival was a senior staff member of the Manchester Royal Infirmary. The existence of the public hospital was, ideologically speaking, proof of the Enlightenment spirit of tending to the needs of the sick and poor. The limited resources granted for its operation, however, showed the limits of this benevolent concern. Under the constraining and strictly regulated circumstances, the three main professional groups of the hospital, physicians, surgeons, and apothecaries, entered an internal struggle for the scarce resources that led in 1791 to the closure of the typhoid ward, while the epidemic was still rampant.[11]

Percival was called upon to devise rules by which the command chains and the division of labor could be clarified to avoid similar mishaps in the future. The result was his book, at manuscript stage titled "Medical Jurisprudence." Since many ethics books on proper medical conduct preceded Percival's work and since it could not be officially elevated to the status of law, commentators have suggested that "Medical Etiquette" would have been the correct name.[12] Be that as it may, Percival's reputation was cemented when the American Medical Association adopted its own code of conduct in 1847, citing him as the main source of inspiration. The legacy lives on in the World Medical Association's declarations, a constantly evolving corpus updating the Hippocratic oath and leaning on subsequent codes of medical, healthcare, and research ethics.[13]

The organization of public healthcare continued, partly as a result of wartime hardship. In the United States, the Civil War casualties prompted the establishment of army hospitals in the North;[14] and Florence Nightingale's efforts during the Crimean War professionalized nursing and furthered for its part the use of statistics in care provision and public health policy.[15]

At the end of the nineteenth century, the discovery and scientific recognition of microorganisms led to advances in antisepsis and disease control in health-care practice and to the emergence of bacteriology and microbiology in research. Vaccines started to curb pandemics and inventions like pasteurization began to have some impact on nutritional safety.[16] Contagious diseases continued to be a threat in both times of peace and times of war, though.

2.2 Political, Economic, and Ideological Concerns

While the principles of beneficence, nonmaleficence, dignity, vulnerability, and perhaps solidarity spontaneously emerge from healthcare and research practices, other rules pertinent to bioethics seem to emanate from more political, economic, and ideological concerns. The introduction of social equality in the aftermath of the French Revolution, for instance, can be interpreted as a moral advance that had a solid economic foundation. The new industrial order of capitalism required a fit and compliant workforce, and both reformists and moderate conservatives were quick to realize the value of a healthy and obedient population.

The publication of Charles Darwin's *On the Origin of Species* in 1859 gradually led to the acceptance of the theory of biological evolution. This was a scientific turning point, but it also gave rise to eugenics, a political movement that had more to do with racism and elitism than with medicine or biology.[17] The idea was simple. If the survival of the fittest applies to humans – and why would it not? – then it stands to reason that some people adapt to their environment better than others. Insofar as this is hereditary, the more adaptive ones would also produce more adaptive offspring, at least if the circumstances remain the same. This much is noncontroversial, although due to the "insofar" and "if" caveats also well-nigh inapplicable.

The limitations of the model did not stop the champions of eugenics from claiming that they could pinpoint the groups of people who were fit and who were unfit and suggesting that only the fit should be encouraged to have children. This adaptation of individuals to the environment would spare the cost of improving the environment. They then went on, unerringly, to identify their own ethnic, gender, socioeconomic, and faith groups as fit and others unfit. I will dissect some of the ramifications of their thinking later (Section 8), but here it suffices to note the appeal to utility and justice in public health policy. If the aim is to have a healthy workforce, for both individual and collective benefit, then preventing ill health and antisocial behavior by preselection should be, unless other factors contradict this, as good as building public hospitals and arranging moral education.

Termination of pregnancies would have been the most natural route for the eugenicists to take, but abortion, previously legal till quickening in many countries, had come under pressure during the nineteenth century, for an array of related and unrelated reasons.[18] Medical scientists pointed out that the traditional demarcation was arbitrary. Quickening identifies the time when the woman first feels the fetus move in her womb, but this is not an indication of its developmental status. The observation paved the way for the belief that the new human life is present and sacrosanct from "the moment of conception" – in itself an inaccurate description of the process of embryonic growth, but a potent rhetoric tool.

The emphasis on science hid the political motivations underlying the attack against the availability of abortion. Women's liberation was on the rise – Mary Wollstonecraft, Elizabeth Barrett Browning, Lucretia Mott, Elizabeth Cady Stanton, and George Eliot, among others, were eagerly read – and the regulation was a part of the backlash against it. Racists and later on eugenicists had worries about White Anglo-Saxon Protestant women terminating their pregnancies while Catholic and African American women continued to have large families. And, perhaps most importantly, medical doctors, a profession still fighting for status and authority, wanted to get rid of the by now often efficient and inexpensive competition provided by midwives and pharmacists.[19]

As confidence in science grew, the treatment of mental ailments also underwent radical changes. Behavioral and intellectual differences that had once been regarded as a matter of divine intervention and then a question of morality were now classified as physiological failures, some caused by external factors and others by inherited degeneration. Asylums were established, treatments were compulsory and often invasive, and the mentally ill came to be seen as a medically classifiable subpopulation of their own.[20]

In terms of bioethics, a long way off yet, these developments gave us the principle of sanctity of life, with its adjacent doctrine of double effect,[21] the practice of strong scientific and medical paternalism, a racist, eugenic, and antifeminist ideology, the medicalization of mental differences, and the denial of women's personal autonomy as well as their professional and vocational self-rule in healthcare. These elements continued to brew through modernization, revolutions, and two world wars, and in the end produced the issues that bioethics as an academic discipline took up.

Medical ethics up until the 1960s stressed the authority of the physician, the importance of confidentiality and a good bedside manner, and the wrongness of contraception and terminations of pregnancies. The principles of beneficence and nonmaleficence, as well as a strong sense of duty, were in evidence, as was a pronatalist interpretation of the dignity and sanctity of human life. Patient autonomy, especially in the case of women, did not have a place in this medical morality. Continuing the eugenic tradition, forced sterilizations of the mentally challenged and Indigenous groups continued to be a practice. The doctor knew best.

Research ethics, or, to be more precise, failures in research ethics, made the first dent in the physicians' armor. Nazi doctors who participated in euthanasia programs and conducted scientifically questionable and often cruel experiments on nonconsenting prisoners in concentration camps and elsewhere were exposed in the aftermath of the Second World War and put on trial by the victorious Allied forces in 1947 in Nuremberg. In the case *United States of America* v. *Karl Brandt, et al.* before a US military court, twenty medical doctors and three others were accused of involvement in human experiments and mass murder, and most of them were sentenced to death or imprisonment.[22] Although the war crimes trials, of which this was the first one, met jurisprudential criticism, it became clear that not all doctors can always be trusted to know best.

The verdicts were retrospective and, as such, against a strict reading of the rule of law, which states that no one should be convicted of deeds that were not illegal when they were committed. As a way around this, the war crimes tribunal assumed a natural law position (some basic precepts are valid law even in the absence of their recognition by existing legislation). They stated that although some "experiments yield results for the good of society that are unprocurable by other methods or means of study" there must still be limitations to permissible experimentation. These were encapsulated in the ten principles of the Nuremberg Code, the first of which states: "The voluntary consent of the human subject is absolutely essential."[23]

Although the Code started a process that led to our twenty-first-century regulations, medical researchers in the United States did not feel that it had anything to do with their work. A bunch of evil Nazi doctors had been punished, which was good and proper, but since decent physicians and scientists in civilized countries would not commit such crimes, there was no special message for them.[24] In fact, the Code's concentration on individuals and their "absolutely essential" consent was seen as a potential hindrance to work done in medical research and practice.[25]

In research, this attitude enabled, among other things, the 1932-initiated Tuskegee Syphilis Study to continue until 1972, although the experiment on African American men involved sustained lying and a systematic failure to provide the subjects with proper medical treatment, both offenses under the Nuremberg Code.[26] In the self-regulation of medical practice, the mindset was well expressed in the 1947 Geneva Declaration by the World Medical

Association.[27] This rewriting of the Hippocratic oath asserted the authority of the physician and sent seekers of medical help back to their place as passive recipients of treatment and care. Respect for patient autonomy, the research requirement of the Nuremberg Code, only entered the Geneva Declaration as an amendment in 2017.[28]

3 Bioethics as an Academic Discipline

3.1 The Emergence of the New Field of Inquiry in the United States

Bioethics in its practical guises – professional self-regulation, national legislation, policy, and international agreements and declarations – has, then, been around for millennia and continues to be so. The focus here, however, is on a more recent phenomenon, namely the systematic academic reflection and investigation of medical, healthcare, and research practices from the viewpoint of morality. In this sense, the discipline saw the light of day in the United States in the late 1960s.

Albert Jonsen's 1998 description of its beginnings is representative of at least one prominent path from theology and philosophy into the world of medicine.[29] His personal story was that, as a young Jesuit theologian, he first became aware through his tutor that something was sizzling in biology and then happened to encounter medical professionals who introduced him to practical yet theoretically intriguing end-of-life issues. These included dialysis suicide and brain death. As to the first, some patients were so weary of being dependent on kidney machines that they wanted to discontinue the treatment. This did not suit the ethos of their physicians, so the psychopathology of ending one's life by refusing dialysis was considered. As to the second, brain death became an issue with developments in transplantation surgery and the concurrent shortage of good-quality organs. If surgeons waited until the dying patient's heartbeat stopped, damage to the organs was possible. They needed a criterion of death that would allow them to go to work earlier. This was found in the definition of death as the cessation of certain higher or lower brain functions.[30]

Interestingly for my narrative, Jonsen goes on to recount how ethical problems abounded at the time on a national level in the United States. The civil rights movement was much to the fore and the war in Southeast Asia raised questions about justified warfare and the citizens' duty to observe laws and be involved in government actions that they do not condone. Many philosophers who later on came to be recognized as bioethicists were involved in academic discussions on conscientious objection[31] and civil disobedience.[32] Owing to his own background, Jonsen was particularly aware of the clash between the exemptions from military service granted to members of "peace churches,"

Quakers and Mennonites, but not to Catholics, whose teaching included the legitimacy of some wars.[33]

Many justice-related public affairs topics were for a while debated side by side with abortion, euthanasia, and other medicine-related moral issues in journals of applied philosophy. In addition to civil rights and civil disobedience, they included environmental matters and the position of women.[34] As bioethics in the United States evolved and specialized, however, these were sidelined or became fields of inquiry of their own. Feminist concerns were never absent from bioethics – debates on abortion and reproductive technologies saw to that. Distinctly feminist approaches to bioethics, however, took a while to develop and to become an independent branch of the discipline. Environmental ethics, in its turn, rapidly developed into a separate subfield. As the story of this treatise unfolds, I will suggest that this could and maybe should be partly reversed. There is a connection that was lost but can be found again.

The questions that Jonsen saw as focal to the new field included, in his words: "What is benefit? What is harm? Who should live? Who should die? How should the expensive resources of health care be distributed? Who should decide?"[35] These questions are indicative of the life-and-death issues that drew the attention of the majority of bioethicists during the last decades of the twentieth century. Abortion, euthanasia, and decision-making under scarcity loomed large, and benefits and harms needed to be redefined, the relationship between healers and their clientele recalibrated, and rules of distributive justice reconsidered.[36]

An important principle in the abortion and euthanasia debates was respect for autonomy. Liberals argued that women and the terminally ill should be allowed to decide what happens in and to their bodies, as should all healthcare customers who had previously been in the iron grip of medical paternalism. Here the requirement of informed consent, which had started its medical life as a securer of compliance in amputations and seemed to appear out of the blue in the Nuremberg Code, was extended to healthcare more generally. The traditional idea of patients surrendering their self-rule in exchange for healing benefits was upended, and not initially for reasons related to professional self-regulation. Society had changed, individualism had gained ground, and the legal ideas of privacy and personal rights were ready to be applied to new fields. As time went by, with the rise of medical consumerism and the litigation culture, autonomy and informed consent became tools of self-defense for physicians, but that was a later development. At the time, conservatives were quick to respond that concentration on individual autonomy can go against the dignity and sanctity of human life and fail to take into account vulnerability, lack of decisional capacity, and duties to self and others.[37]

Toward the end of the 1970s, bioethics was ready to evolve from case-by-case debates to a more methodical tactic. Jonsen and his fellow Catholic thinkers Edmund Pellegrino[38] and David Thomasma[39] opted for casuistry and virtues, leaning on the idea that particular medical situations will reveal their moral features to diligent observers. A different approach was offered first by the Belmont Report issued in 1978[40] and then by Tom Beauchamp and James Childress's seminal *Principles of Biomedical Ethics* a year later.[41]

All the ethical concerns that had emerged from various sources during the millennia were addressed in the – still authoritative – Belmont Report, although they were formally condensed into three principles for research on humans: respect for persons, beneficence, and justice. Respect for persons includes protection of autonomy, treatment with courtesy and respect, procuring informed consent, truthfulness, and the avoidance of deception, so it is a principle of self-rule, dignity, and general decency all in one. Beneficence means maximizing the good that comes out of the research project while ensuring that the risks to the research subjects are minimized, and "Do no harm" is cited as its background philosophy, so it is also a principle of non-maleficence and vulnerability. Justice requires that research procedures are reasonable, nonexploitative, and well considered and that they are administered fairly as far as costs and benefits to potential research participants are concerned and equally. Vulnerability gets more attention here in the ban on exploitation. The fair distribution of costs and benefits is confined to potential research participants, excluding social utility. What is reasonable, well considered, and equal is left open to interpretation, or thought to be self-evident. The more philosophical dimensions of the principles are, in any case, a moot point, because in practice the Report's message is "only" that scientists have to secure or consider securing informed consent, conduct a risk–benefit assessment, and pay attention to the selection of subjects of research.

Beauchamp and Childress (the latter was one of the drafters of the Belmont Report) extended the principles from research governance to the entire field of biomedical ethics and separated the two consequence-related rules. Accordingly, they ended up with the principles of autonomy, beneficence, nonmaleficence, and justice. Their doctrine has ever since set the tone of bioethics in the United States and elsewhere, especially where the discipline has evolved into a profession. Ethical practitioners working within healthcare institutions have found good use for a model that does not require too much theorizing or full casuistic inquiries into patients' situations.

The principlist approach has received its share of criticism, but it is not always clear how justified the objections are. Beauchamp and Childress's 1979 rendition was already so detailed and nuanced that most alternative takes on bioethics can be explained in its terms. Subsequent editions have filled whatever gaps the original had and Ruth Macklin's *Against Relativism* clarified the message further by extending it directly to global and feminist concerns.[42] Since the principles are, however, usually adopted in their simplest form, without deep background reflections, two differences between the Belmont Report's ethos and the four-principles model stand out. The Report's respect for persons somehow automatically includes elements of human dignity, vulnerability, and decency that are, at least without further elaboration, missing from the principle of autonomy. And the Report's account of justice, although opaque at times, seems to allow more dimensions than Beauchamp and Childress's fair distribution of burdens and benefits. (More on these in Sections 4 and 5.)

3.2 The Global Coming of Age of Bioethics

Philosophical bioethics had from early on two separate yet intertwined objects of study, namely issues and theory. Judith Jarvis Thomson,[43] Mary Ann Warren,[44] Mary Mothersill,[45] and Philippa Foot,[46] among others, presented views for and against abortion and euthanasia, and the argumentation was often based on imaginary examples and fragments of moral doctrines as used by the author's opponents. This "trolley problem" tactic is still in use in today's bioethics. Others, including Jonsen, Pellegrino, Thomasma, Beauchamp, and Childress, tried to construct theories or approaches that would consistently cover all areas of medicine and healthcare. In terms of justification, the strategies can produce different results. In a single-topic debate, the main argument against abortion was often sanctity of life, but since this doctrine has a limited religious base, casuists and virtue ethicists preferred rationales that could more easily meet secular approval. Similarly, one major argument for the availability of abortion was that the fetus is not a person in a psychological sense, and hence not a holder of human rights yet. Again, this is a theoretically demanding view, which is why autonomy (women's right to choose) and nonmaleficence (eliminating dangerous backstreet abortions) were likelier choices for principlists.

In other English-speaking countries, Peter Singer,[47] Deane Wells,[48] Helga Kuhse,[49] and Paola Cavalieri[50] in Australia and Jonathan Glover[51] and John Harris[52] in England combined the approaches. Their more or less outcome-based, or utilitarian, ethics provided them with a tool for assessing the morality of abortion and euthanasia but also worldwide social and moral issues like famine and poverty, violence and terrorism, and the treatment of nonhuman animals in research and industrial food production; as well as upcoming or more tangentially bioethical concerns like reproductive technologies, infanticide, and systematically harvesting organs for transplantation. This approach received heavy criticism, as Rosalind Hursthouse,[53] Onora O'Neill,[54] Anne Maclean,[55] Eva Feder Kittay,[56] David Oderberg,[57] and Jennifer Jackson[58] argued that the utilitarian framework eliminates genuine morality from medicine and health-care. In a sense, the exchange was a rerun of an earlier debate between J. J. C. Smart and Bernard Williams on the pros and cons of utilitarianism,[59] with reminiscences of Elizabeth Anscombe's anticonsequentialism in the mix.[60]

The tight connection that has existed between theoretical bioethics and medical practice in the United States from the beginning has not been a global phenomenon. Raanan Gillon introduced the four-principle model to England under the title philosophical medical ethics,[61] and through medical school curricula, Beauchamp and Childress's main ideas are now known all over the world. The link with philosophy is tenuous, though, and the principles and their background are not that well understood. This is not a criticism. Even superficially applied, they offer a good checklist. It is just a reminder that insofar as bioethics has turned into a professional practice, it has, worldwide, joined forces with law and the social sciences more than with philosophy.

The 1980s and the 1990s saw a development that is crucial to my quest for justice in bioethics. During this heyday of individual freedom, medical paternalism came under scrutiny by philosophers. The idea of self-rule or autonomy, which had been introduced to medicine and healthcare as if by accident in the Nuremberg Code and its subsequent documents, was now explicitly set against the background of liberal political theories and their rivals. Childress showed how paternalism is at the root of most ethical issues in medicine and healthcare,[62] John Kleinig identified other areas in which the same problem persisted,[63] and Heta Häyry presented a balanced conceptual analysis of freedom and autonomy and their limitations in terms of the person's own good (paternalism), prevailing morality (moralism), and reason (prudentialism).[64]

For liberal bioethicists, autonomy was an easy principle to apply to abortion, euthanasia, the doctor–patient relationship, and public health policies that did not take individuals adequately into account. There were other prominent topics, though, and the questions they raised were different. Many of them became, directly or indirectly, matters of justice.

As medicine could do more and more to keep patients alive and healthy, the scarcity of resources rose to the forefront. Who will be treated first? This is not something to be solved by any standard liberal account of autonomy. When too many people want the same service, they either have to fight for it or rules need to be set to strike a fair and palatable balance. But how? A famous precedent was set by the Seattle Artificial Kidney Center at the University of Washington in the 1960s and the early 1970s. In theory, everything was done by the book.

There was a procedure in place, the community was involved, and a carefully selected committee was in charge of deciding who should receive dialysis treatment and who should not. In practice, the arrangement produced results that were not universally accepted. Scout leaders and Sunday school teachers tended to be included, while beatniks and women with bad reputations did not. A closer look revealed that the conservative middle-class members of the anonymous committees smuggled their own values into the decisions. Philosophers offered more systematic solutions to the questions of justice in the distribution of scarce medical resources.[65]

The appearance of Acquired Immunodeficiency Syndrome (AIDS) in the 1980s was a novel threat to humanity, but also an opportunity for bioethics.[66] Epidemics had been experienced since time immemorial, but the new academic discipline had emerged during a period when people in affluent countries had lulled themselves into believing that advances in medicine had made pestilences a thing of the past. Public authorities and ethicists had to rethink the respective obligations of individuals and society as well as the role of majority- and minority-group memberships in the formation of identities. Straightforward Enlightenment individualism had to give way to the recognition of collectives and communities as building blocks of humanity and agency. Many feminist and postcolonial bioethicists were eager to take this route,[67] as were, later, conservative and nationalist communitarians.

Cloning and genetics were issues that had fermented longer but only fully entered the limelight toward the end of the 1990s.[68] Scientists had already started cloning animals in the nineteenth century by splitting them into two at early stages of their development. The idea of duplicating living beings more delicately, however, had attracted the minds of researchers and science fiction writers since the 1920s. At the time when bioethics was born, Nobel Laureate for Physiology and Medicine Joshua Lederberg suggested that cloning and genetic engineering would be excellent instruments for improving the human race.[69] Two Protestant theologians, Paul Ramsey and Joseph Fletcher, were among the first to react, Ramsey criticizing and Fletcher defending Lederberg's view.

Ramsey's condemnation of cloning and associated genetic alterations was based on Christian values. He argued that condoning technologies like these would promote an overly hedonistic view of human happiness, a dangerously individualistic and calculating view of morality, and a mistakenly disembodied and nonsexual view of personhood. In other words, it would mean the end of the world as conservative Christians of his kind knew it.[70] This introduced into bioethics the idea that holding on to traditional ways of life can be desirable in and by itself.

Fletcher represented the opposite stance, arguing that change would be good. Preference satisfaction is the cornerstone of happiness; planning and calculation are good; and individuals are rational beings who should be allowed to decide for themselves how they want to produce their children.[71] The consequentialist version of this credo has since been reiterated by many liberal ethicists, and the view has also been dressed up as a theory of genetic justice.[72]

As respect for autonomy, one of the presumptions of Fletcher's argument, can be interpreted in more than one way, its correct reading in the context of genetics and reproduction has been debated. In an exchange, Rosamond Rhodes defended a substantive Kantian doctrine of rational self-rule,[73] while Tuija Takala countered this with a thinner Millian idea of freedom to do what one wishes.[74]

In an early contribution to the cloning discussion, Ruth Chadwick presented in 1982 the outcome-based justification in a slightly different light. She cataloged and dutifully rejected the arguments from unnaturalness, normal functioning, playing God, rights to genetic uniqueness and privacy, worthwhile lives, preferences, and side effects on society and on the gene pool. She added, however, some snide observations which partly reverse the message. These targeted the standard utilitarian reliance on technology and the doctrine's nonchalance in the face of uncertain social and political consequences.[75] The observations, which amount to a criticism of both cloning and consequentialism, tally with my own thoughts on bioethics, morality, and utilitarianism (of which more in Section 9).[76]

4 Two Takes on Justice in Bioethics

4.1 American Principles

Healthcare practice, biomedical research, and social developments have, then, given rise to a wide array of doctrines and principles that bioethics as an academic discipline can utilize. Justice in some sense is a standard element in all methods of assessing medicine and adjacent fields from the viewpoint of morality. It is, however, interpreted differently by different schools of thought. The principlist model sees it primarily as a mechanism for distributing burdens and benefits fairly and equitably. I will call the view reflected in the model the "American principles" approach, fully aware that there is more to the Americas than the United States, that not everybody in the United States roots for it, and that similar lines of thinking can be found all over the world.[77] This is a matter of terminological convenience, as I will in the next section (4.2) contrast it with "European values," evoking similar caveats.

My considerations in this section are based on the situation at the turn of the millennium. That is as far as my narrative has proceeded and, since bioethics is a historically evolving beast, it is useful to take interim stock of the situation at the point when the "European" challenge to the "American" model began to be launched. The upshot is, of course, that my first thesis will get, for now, only limited support, but I will complete the defense in later sections. Several continental plates in international and ethical thinking were moving at the time and taking this into account will be essential for my effort.

Beauchamp and Childress, in their 2001 edition of *Principles of Biomedical Ethics*, rightly note that justice has formal and material dimensions. Formal justice requires that equals "must be treated equally, and unequals must be treated unequally":[78] To everyone what is due to them. Material justice specifies the bases on which dues are assigned. Beauchamp and Childress list six such bases: "To each person an equal share;" "To each person according to need;" "To each person according to effort;" "To each person according to contribution;" "To each person according to merit;" "To each person according to free market exchanges." They submit that these often contradict one another and that they may apply differently to different cases.[79]

Beauchamp and Childress go on to describe four philosophical theories on what persons are due:

> *Utilitarian* theories emphasize a mixture of criteria for the purpose of maximizing public utility; *libertarian* theories emphasize rights to social and economic liberty (invoking fair procedures rather than substantive outcomes); *communitarian* theories stress the principles and practices of justice that evolve through traditions and practices in a community; and *egalitarian* theories emphasize equal access to the goods of life that every rational person values (often invoking material criteria of need and equality).[80]

Both the range of theories and their depictions and criticisms are telling.

Utilitarianism, according to Beauchamp and Childress, requires us to maximize value or overall good or net social utility (these are all the same to them). No rights exist independently of this requirement. A utilitarian government would probably secure us our basic healthcare, and even grant that we have a right to it, but the right would not be natural or based on our individuality or personhood or agency. It would be based on the contingent fact that the existence of such a right is conducive to the greatest social utility. For Beauchamp and Childress, this is problematic, "because social utility could change at any time" and then the right would cease to exist. Another criticism they raise is that the "sickest and most vulnerable populations" could, under a utility-maximizing regime, be left untended to.[81]

Libertarianism is an embodiment of the free-market spirit that has been prevalent in the United States. It holds that individuals have rights to their life and physical integrity against assault, and to private property. The government's function is to protect these by a system of law enforcement and criminal justice, but the state's influence should extend no further. A publicly financed healthcare system based on progressive taxation would be coercive and unjust. Taking money from property owners and spending it on healthcare for others would violate the property owners' rights. Healthcare should be for those who can pay for it, either directly or, through a voluntary insurance system, indirectly. Beauchamp and Childress note that the view is quite uncompromising and that "communitarian and egalitarian theories have offered influential challenges."[82]

Communitarians reject models of society that are based on rights, contracts, or utility calculations. For them, the political system that has developed spontaneously and from within is the most natural and the one that should be observed and cherished. Beauchamp and Childress give three examples of this kind of thinking. In the Netherlands, the entire political system is based on solidarity as an alternative to or reading of social justice. The poor, the disabled, and the vulnerable have priority in healthcare, and this is said to be based on the inborn Dutch ethos. Another way would be to organize civil action on a local level. In this model, "small deliberative democratic communities" would "develop shared conceptions of the good life and justice." And yet another way is to look harder into the already prevailing ideals and note their clashes with official policies. The United States, for instance, could be morally ready to move beyond the two-tier healthcare system of "a decent minimum for all and then liberty of contract for the advantaged."[83]

Egalitarianism demands equal shares at least when it comes to the most important constituents of well-being. Beauchamp and Childress quickly note, however, that "no prominent egalitarian theory requires equal sharing of all possible benefits" and then revert to Rawlsian language by saying that a qualified form of the creed "requires only some basic equalities among individuals, and permits inequalities that redound to the benefit of the least advantaged." John Rawls had defended this view in *A Theory of Justice*, arguing that rational decision-makers who do not know what their own assets are would choose this kind of arrangement for the political environment in which they would prefer to live. Basic goods for all, equality of opportunity, and, after that, individuals can improve their lot as much as they can, provided that those who are in the worst positions in society also benefit from the system that allows these inequalities.[84]

With this turn, the American Principles approach opens a new front in the discussion on justice. Norman Daniels, building on Rawlsian ideas, focuses on the fair equality of opportunity and makes it the cornerstone of healthcare ethics. It is not only about the distribution of resources for treating traumas and curing diseases but also about having the chance to avoid mishap and illness before they even occur. The attention shifts from "access to health care to the social determinants of health outcomes." The idea is that wider social justice would also lead to better health in the population.[85]

Fair equality of opportunity has many interpretations, and some of them can be quite far-reaching. Beauchamp and Childress cite Rawls describing his position and note that if we follow his line of thought the entire United States social and healthcare system should be rebuilt. All radical inequalities should be removed unless they somehow serve the least advantaged. Against this, libertarians have argued that a line must be drawn between disadvantages that are unfair (these need to be removed) and those that are "merely" unfortunate (these need not). Beauchamp and Childress hover somewhere between these, recognizing the inadequacy of the libertarian solution in issues of rationing but also acknowledging the uncertain practical implications of the Rawlsian view.[86]

In a timely contribution in 2000, Daniels, together with Allen Buchanan, Dan W. Brock, and Daniel Wikler, applied moral and political considerations to emerging technologies in *From Chance to Choice: Genetics and Justice*. They dissected and renounced earlier forms of eugenics, arguing that their main problem was in the paternalistic and coercive ethos. The problem, they seemed to allege, could be solved by letting people make autonomous reproductive choices. In these, genetic selection, with proper social precautions, could have a beneficial role. If parents chose to avoid hereditary diseases in their offspring, many disadvantages would never even come into being.[87] Jamie Lindemann Nelson and Hilde Lindemann Nelson, among others, pointed out that there are feminist and disability considerations that could produce objections to this "new eugenics."[88]

Critics of the American Principles model had several complaints. They saw its inherent individualism as a threat to collective commitments which keep communities and societies going and are essential to human flourishing. They repelled its thin concept of freedom as the absence of coercion and constraint which they saw contributing to hedonistic consumerism. And they resented its alleged neutrality in the face of substantive values which they saw as a smokescreen for the American ideology (whatever that is) invading medical, healthcare, and research ethics all over the world.[89]

Some of these criticisms are more legitimate than others, but they all have their roots in the original justification that Beauchamp and Childress offered for

the theory. Their argument was that the principles of autonomy, nonmaleficence, beneficence, and justice are supported by deontological (duty-based) and
consequentialist (outcome-oriented) moral views, and since these exhaust
rational and reasonable views on ethics, the rules are valid everywhere and at
all times. Although they later on forsook this stance and now claim that the
principles emerge from a universal common morality,[90] the damage, from the
viewpoint of skeptics, had already been done.

Although it was customary in late 1970s English-speaking philosophical
circles to think that deontology, as expressed by Immanuel Kant and other
Christian ethicists, and utilitarianism, as initially formulated by Jeremy
Bentham and John Stuart Mill, covered the entire realm of moral theory, my
story so far has already revealed a third alternative. It is virtue ethics, based on the
teleological philosophy of Aristotle in Greek antiquity, developed by Thomas
Aquinas in medieval Europe, and applied to bioethics by Catholic theologians
from the birth of the discipline. With the work of Alasdair MacIntyre, especially
his *After Virtue* in 1981,[91] the doctrine started to spread among secular academia,
as well, and in the 2001 edition it is already well covered by Beauchamp and
Childress. Not everyone was reading the latest version, though. Rightly or
wrongly, the impression persisted that principlism focuses on a liberal reading
of autonomy,[92] hails the right of individuals to do what they wish, ignores moral
and religious virtues, and denies any need to think about the ideal nature of good
human beings.

4.2 European Values

Bioethics – as opposed to medical ethics, healthcare ethics, nursing ethics,
professional ethics, research ethics, applied ethics, and the like – arrived in the
United Kingdom with Gillon's *Philosophical Medical Ethics* during the 1980s.[93]
It then proceeded gradually to the rest of Europe, albeit that all through the 1990s
the term was in German-speaking countries associated with Peter Singer, whose
utilitarian views were very unpopular.[94] As a reaction, partly to Singer and his
fellow "bioutilitarians" Glover and Harris and partly to the "Americanness"
linked with Beauchamp and Childress, there was a sense that European ethicists
should identify their own principles. These would be based on "European Values"
and signal more clearly the concerns that were (seen to be) left unanswered by
Beauchamp and Childress's principles of autonomy, nonmaleficence, beneficence, and justice. Ideally, they would emphasize more prominently prudence,
communality, and the intrinsic morality of human actions.

During 1995–8, the European Commission funded a collaborative project in
which Peter Kemp and his twenty-one partners from various European countries were tasked with bringing clarity to the issue. They investigated the

primary values that could serve as a basis for ethically sound decision-making in medicine, healthcare, and research. In the final meeting of the project, sixteen participants issued a document named the Barcelona Declaration, in which they identified four fundamental principles: autonomy, dignity, integrity, and vulnerability.[95]

Dignity became the paramount consideration in the Declaration. The idea was that although autonomy (in the American Principles sense) is important, bioethics and biolaw need more because there are human beings who are not self-ruling in the first place. Concentration on informed choice would exclude embryos, fetuses, infants, the comatose, the severely cognitively challenged, the demented, and the senile. These groups must be protected by respect for human dignity, complemented and qualified by the notions of integrity and vulnerability.

Kemp and his group's disagreement with and departure from the American Principles can be seen in their description of autonomy:

> Autonomy is not only to be interpreted in the liberal sense as "permission". Rather, five important meanings of autonomy can be put forward: 1) autonomy as capacity of creation of ideas and goals for life, 2) autonomy as capacity of moral insight, 3) autonomy as capacity of decision and action with lack of outer constraints, 4) autonomy as capacity of political involvement and personal responsibility, 5) autonomy as capacity of informed consent. Autonomy should be considered as a principle of the self-legislation of rational human beings taking part in the same human lifeworld. This does not exclude the recognition of pluralism as a political fact of modern society. But it is necessary to work with a more comprehensive idea of autonomy, recognising the tensions between different conceptions of the good. The republican sense of autonomy is based on the vision of "the good life for and with the other in just institutions". This vision is put forward as the basis for privacy, confidentiality and informed consent.[96]

In their haste to denounce the "liberal view of autonomy as permission," the group may have partly engaged in a battle against strawmen. Apart from moral insight and political involvement, all the listed senses can probably be found in Beauchamp and Childress, and even those could be read into the Belmont Report's respect for persons. Kemp and partners do, however, also identify a clash that is real.

There are bioethicists, American and non-American, who would like to keep moral and political views completely out of their discipline and its take on justice. Rawls famously argued for the neutrality of the state – that it should not take sides in people's disagreements concerning the good life. The 2001 version of Beauchamp and Childress seems to align with this. There are, however, also bioethicists, European and non-European, who would like to explicitly include moral and political views in their discipline's fundamental principles. Insofar as we are talking about the opposition against the American four-principles model, the stress is on the word "explicitly." The underlying claim is that ideology is always present in ethics and that the allegedly neutral liberal approach is in fact itself a substantive code – one of amorality and license.

The critics of neutrality can be called "republican" in contrast with the "liberal" alternative. Individuals are preceded by and subdued to a res publica, a public body, which defines their proper being. Or, in the group's words, there is a "tension between the human existence as an unencumbered self and the embodied, embedded, character of human experience." Liberal autonomy is not sufficient, because we "must recognise the human person as a situated subject."[97] In light of this, I could have called the two takes on bioethics and justice liberal and republican, but since these words have unnecessarily limiting political connotations, I will stick to American and European, with proper caveats. It is not really a geographic distinction, but we know that.

To supplement even their own inclusive view on autonomy, the group stressed the role of dignity, which they saw as an intrinsic value, the cornerstone of morality in human relationships, and a reminder of the inviolability of human life. They went on to state that human dignity as an intersubjective concept has seven dimensions:

> 1) It expresses the intrinsic value of the human being in a community or society. 2) It includes respect for the moral agency of the human subject. 3) It means that every human being must be considered as being without price and unable to be commercialised. 4) This includes that human dignity refers to the indeterminant position of human beings in the universe. 5) Self-esteem, proudness, shame, feeling of inferiority and degradation are essentially matters of human dignity expressed in the intersubjective relations between individuals. 6) Dignity can establish restrictions on interventions in human beings in taboo-situations, because of the necessity of human civilised behaviour. 7) Finally, dignity relates to metaphysical experiences of human beings in existential limit by degrading treatment.[98]

In conclusion to their summary, the group state that human dignity is also the basis of human rights, as it "expresses the intrinsic worth and fundamental equality of all human beings."[99] This legal, or international agreement, turn brings the European view close to the United Nations (UN) Universal Declaration of Human Rights (more on this in Section 7).

To make yet more distinct the departure from permissive liberal individualism, the principle of integrity, in the group's view, "refers to the totality of life saying that it should not be destroyed" and "a coherence that in a certain sense must not be touched." Still, almost returning to the four-principles themes of autonomy, and certainly to the Belmont Report's respect for persons, they give four meanings to the concept:

> 1) Integrity as a narrative totality, wholeness, completeness. 2) Integrity as a personal sphere of self-determination. 3) Integrity as a virtue of uncorrupted character, expressing uprightness, honesty and good character. 4) Integrity as a legal notion, where it expresses the moral coherence of the legal or medical system.[100]

While the second meaning could be regarded as a liberal reading of personal self-rule, the first introduces a more metaphysical understanding of personhood, the third echoes the decency required by the Belmont Report, and the fourth rises above individual concerns and makes integrity a matter of the public body at the level of legislatures and healthcare institutions. The "totality of life" aspect also means that the scope of application is not necessarily anthropocentric but could be extended to nonhuman animals and organic existence more generally. Although the group does not develop this idea to its conclusion, this is significant to my narrative later on (Section 9).

Respect for vulnerability marks what is possibly the deepest difference between the "American" and "European" models. Autonomy can be defined thickly or thinly; dignity, for the part that concerns medical ethics, can perhaps be covered by beneficence and nonmaleficence; and integrity can, give or take the republican metaphysics, be embraced by self-rule and decency. Attitudes concerning vulnerability, however, make the distinction impenetrable. It is something that the four principles and adjacent philosophies would like to eradicate or alleviate. Not so according to Kemp and his partners, who say:

> Vulnerability should be considered as a universal expression of the human condition. Moreover, it appeals to protection of both animals and the teleological auto-organisation of the world. However, vulnerability has been largely misunderstood in modern society, which has been guided by a socalled vulnerability reducing agenda, which aims to eliminate all vulnerability, i.e. suffering, abnormality, deafness and disability, in order to create perfect human beings. Respect for vulnerability must find the right balance between this logic of struggle for immortality and the finitude of the earthly presence of human suffering. As an expression of the destiny of finitude the moral receptivity of vulnerability, i.e. the disclosure of the vulnerability of the other, is the foundation of ethics in our time.[101]

Respect for vulnerability, then, means exactly what it says – recognizing, accepting, and holding on to human frailty, even celebrating it, instead of trying to remove it. This could not be farther away from the new eugenics, flirted with by liberal bioethicists and embraced by bioutilitarians.

Justice is not included in the European Values model as a principle of its own, but when it comes to matters of prioritization in medicine, healthcare, and research, Kemp and his colleagues introduce the idea of solidarity. Their principles of autonomy, dignity, integrity, and vulnerability would form, they argue, the foundation of a new way of evaluating priorities. This can be defined negatively (for what it does not allow) and positively (for what it suggests).

Negatively, solidarity arising from the four European principles does not permit mere utility calculations at any level. Emerging medical technologies should not be assessed only on the basis of their costs and benefits. General healthcare decisions should not lean exclusively on health economic tools like Quality Adjusted Life Years (QALYs). On the latter, Kemp and partners write:

> Even though pragmatic concern for limited resources might be necessary this can also include a lack of moral sensibility, because general health economical prioritisation is mobilised instead of concern for the needs of the individual patient. [The] concern for collective usefulness and rationality means that it is most rational to treat the young before the old, those who have most chance to survive before the weak etc. In the light of respect for human dignity such quantifying descriptions are unjust because they ignore the unique and endless value of each human being. [. . .] Maximisation of common needs is contrary to the protection of the most vulnerable people in society.[102]

The phrases "collective usefulness" and "maximization of common needs" must be taken to stress utility and needs and their transparent calculation, as the group's own views on res publica imply that they are not at all averse to the inclusion of collective and common good as long as it is opaque and can be expressed in their terms. The cited passage simply makes the distinction between utilitarianism and republicanism. (Interestingly, one of the most ardent bioutilitarians, Harris, opposes QALYs for similar reasons, albeit in a different language.)[103]

Positively, solidarity seems to mean simultaneous attention to all of the four principles. In the explanations, the vocabulary grows to include responsibility and care:

> The basic ethical principles are promoted in the framework of solidarity and responsibility. This includes the idea of social progress towards a more developed society. The principles are an expression to the movement of society in the civilising progress towards the Kingdom of Ends. Their application corresponds to the integration of the principles in an ethics of care. It is the task of this ethics to take care of civilisation and secure the self-realisation

of human individuals in the welfare state. This involves that ideas of social insurance should be integrated in a collective responsibility of society. The basic ethical principles in the civilisatory movement constitute a change from a contractual rights claim to a protective rights claim confronted with technological development.[104]

This passage is rich in detail, but one thing stands out. Justice, or solidarity, in the European model means much more than prioritization or distribution of health or other costs and benefits. In a sense, all the principles are principles of justice, or constituents of justice. Seen from this angle, the same holds true about the American model. Let me explain this thought by introducing a map of justice that takes a more comprehensive view on the dimensions of political morality.

5 Varieties of Justice

5.1 Tensions between Political Moralities

The descriptions of the four American and four European principles mention or hint at several political moralities that they either embrace or reject. These include egalitarianism, libertarianism, liberalism, utilitarianism, communitarianism, and care ethics. Between the doctrines, there are similarities and differences, agreements and disagreements that are worth presenting in a systematic form. This will result in a conceptual map of justice, which can then be employed to compare the two takes with one another and with further alternatives (in Section 5.2).[105]

Almost everyone agrees that at the core of justice lies equality. The American and European models of bioethics are no exception to this. Everybody should be seen as equal, everybody should be respected and treated equally and equitably, everyone should be counted as one and no one should be counted as more or less than one in political practices, and all those affected by decisions should be heard or taken into account when the decisions are made.

When it comes to defining equality or giving it substance, however, tensions start to build. Three dimensions stand out: the proper moral foundation and best arrangement of economies, the right way of identifying interests to be accounted for in decisions, and the best basis for assigning and securing opportunities.

5.1.1 Property and Responsibility

Both the American and the European principlist approaches recognize the need for prioritization in distributing scarce medical and healthcare resources. Apart from addressing the issues of need, effort, contribution, merit, utility, and vulnerability, they both make a wider commitment to an economy based on relatively free market exchanges. Beauchamp and Childress shy away from fully-fledged libertarianism but do not doubt the value of privately controlled property (or means of production) and at least some degree of individual responsibility for one's health. Kemp and partners argue along similar lines. They take for granted the moral imperative of a welfare state, but a welfare state is a regulated free-market system. As for responsibility, for all their protestations of giving precedence to the vulnerable, Kemp and partners also seem to think that patients who are decent should be prioritized over those who are indecent or reckless. This detail surfaces in an example they give of resource allocation, and their ethics seems to align with the spirit of the early Seattle dialysis case.[106]

So, both models accept the market economy, in other words the current capitalist system. The alternative, in terms of political morality, would be to denounce the growth-oriented free market and the idea of individual responsibility for one's health and condition. Reasons for such a rejection can be factual or, for want of a better word, ideological.

Factually, the argument against the supremacy of the market is that free exchanges are an illusion. The so-called free market is, in reality, a battleground of competing agencies, and corporations and monopolies make sure that the model advertised by classical economic theory remains a conceptual idealization and an unattainable dream. Ideologically, the radical view is that capitalism will lead to the alienation of the workforce, followed by misery, class awareness, and a revolutionary upheaval that results in the emergence of a classless communist society. Less radical views cite the moral inferiority of unequal power relations in production and consumption and claim that a degree of socialism would be preferable.

As for responsibility, the creed labeled luck egalitarianism maintains that although the individuals' contribution to their own condition should, in theory, be a factor in considering compensations for them, in reality their control over the many social determinants of health is frail. It would therefore be both useless and unfair to blame individuals for many of the misfortunes they meet.[107] Elizabeth Anderson's interpretation emphasized the "in theory" element of this type of thinking and made luck egalitarians a target of antilibertarian criticism.[108] More recently, Johanna Ahola-Launonen has set the record straight by sorting out the twists and turns of this "hijacking of responsibility" saga and by showing that a closer-to-socialist reading of the doctrine is probably safer for theoretical purposes.[109]

5.1.2 Spontaneously Evolved vs. Measurable Interests

The second tension between interpretations of equality concerns what kinds of interests should be taken into account in political decision-making and how these interests should be formulated and assessed. This is primarily a clash between communitarians and utilitarians. Reduced to a question of "whose interests," the former support a limited range of beneficiaries – members of families, communities, nations, societies, or regions. The latter favor a universalist or cosmopolitan approach and want to include at least all human beings regardless of differentiating biological, geographic, or cultural features, and perhaps also nonhuman beings who fulfill certain criteria.

Communitarianism has already been described by Beauchamp and Childress above. Rights, contracts, and utility measurements should not as such be used as the foundation of law or policy-making because the spontaneously developed tradition of nations and regions takes precedence over them. This is based on a specific view of human nature. We are not empty containers into which entitlements or well-being can be poured, but essentially social beings, born into our particular situations, bearing our own burdens, and having our own claims on others. In other words, we are not individuals in the liberal sense. Beauchamp and Childress seem to have their misgivings concerning this kind of thinking.

Kemp and his partners, however, strongly side with it. The first thing they say about dignity, their primary value, is that it "expresses the intrinsic value of the human being in a community or society."[110] In all their principles, they reject the liberal notion of an individual and, even when they mention self-rule, they link it with the universal humanity within us rather than our own ideas of what we should or should not do.[111]

Interestingly, they seem to allow two different paths for the evolvement of spontaneous community rules. One is local and involves national sensibilities, as in the Dutch example cited by Beauchamp and Childress. Solidarity toward the vulnerable is the prevailing ethos in the Netherlands and therefore the historically given justification of their welfare state.[112] The other development is more general, so much so that it could be called universal. It is expressed in the recurring Kantian language of dignity as intrinsic human worth and human rights thinking as its legal expression.

At a glance, these interpretations seem quite wide apart. If what has become the custom in the Netherlands goes, then there would seem to be nothing to stop the rise of a racist or otherwise separatist healthcare system.[113] National resources could be allocated to the "original" Dutch instead of foreigners or the vulnerable. This, however, would go against what Kemp and his colleagues say about human dignity and human rights. These should, at least according to standard readings, apply similarly to all human beings.

The explanation for this apparent discrepancy could be found in deep implicit parochialism. Jürgen Habermas has suggested that the kind of dignity included in the European Values has its roots in the ethical self-understanding of the species, which emerged two and a half millennia ago during the "axial age." It then developed in Europe and reached its full expression in Kant's ethical theory.[114] The idea is the one evoked by Kemp and his partners. We are free and autonomous mental beings (and as such aware and in control of ourselves and our aims) but also valuable and dignified bodily beings (carrying in us an element which is unknown and untouchable even to us).

Whatever the metaphysics involved in this concept of dignity, the interesting detail is that it bridges the gap between local and nearly universal. Dutch tradition is valid for the Dutch. The European concept of dignity is valid for Europeans. That the same concept also happens to be the basis of the UN Universal Declaration is coincidental but possibly a sign that the rest of the world is following in Europe's footsteps. Such a development would seem to be partly evidenced by the third example of communitarianism given by Beauchamp and Childress, according to which the United States healthcare system could be ready to evolve toward a more inclusive welfare state.[115]

Utilitarianism, described in one way and partly condoned by Beauchamp and Childress and vehemently opposed by Kemp's group, initially rules out traditions in the evaluation of interests. The interests to be pursued must ideally be concrete, measurable, calculable, and comparable. The action or policy that produces the greatest net good or the smallest net bad should be chosen, regardless of customary views, including duty and right claims. If it turns out that adherence to some such views or rules is conducive to the best result, they will have indirect support. In any case, the best outcome cannot be defined in terms of an opaque common good or public utility. These belong to a more republican concept of political morality.

5.1.3 Opportunities Based on Individuality vs. Relations

The third tension between views on equality and justice concerns opportunities and the proper basis for assigning and securing them. Beauchamp and Childress take a cautious stand on what they see as unclarity or exaggeration in Rawls and his fair equality of opportunity. Kemp and colleagues hardly address the issue by name, perhaps because they see it as a liberal and individualistic concern that has little bearing on the dignity, integrity, and vulnerability of human beings. They do, however, present thoughts on the matter in their definition of autonomy, and their occasional references to ethics of care throw further light on their position.

An apt starting point for discussing equality of opportunity is libertarian, or classically liberal. As long as no one is prevented, by explicit coercion, from entering lucrative and influential positions in society, everything is in order. Poor childhood conditions, lack of internal drive, and prevailing attitudes can collude to make it more difficult for some than for others to reach the desired positions, but it is not the society's, or especially the state's, role to interfere with this. Some rise, some fall, but that is the way of the world. A eugenicist might add that this is how natural selection works and that any corrective movements would just be a waste of other people's resources and an invitation for the "bad stock" to thrive.

The American and European bioethicists that I have focused on so far are not libertarians, or classical liberals, and they have more humane, or philanthropic, ideas. Since biological and social determinants are not within the reach of individuals, or their fault, a fair and equitable arrangement would include at least some corrections and compensations. Beauchamp and Childress are amenable to the idea of making adjustments in the educational and social conditions so that people with less favorable endowments could get a better chance to succeed in their lives. They do not use the argument, but their view could be supported by the classical liberal credo that freedom, in this case augmented and supported positive freedoms to achieve important things in life, can actually serve public utility, or the benefit of all, as well as individual interests.

The language used by Kemp and company in their definition of autonomy converges with Beauchamp and Childress's recognition of positive freedoms. They go further, though, and include immaterial as well as material values and interests. Genuine autonomy is not only "permission" (negative freedom from explicit coercion and constraints that stop you doing something you otherwise could) but also capacities to create ideas and goals for life, to have moral insight, to engage in politics, and to take personal responsibility. These concerns are almost individualistic and certainly universal.

By repeatedly referring to care and ethics of care, Kemp and his partners emphasize the communal and relational side of their model. This creates a possible tension with the capacity considerations, but as they do not elaborate on their particular reading of the ethics of care, it is best to discuss this in the next section, in the framework of the map of justice that can be built around the three dimensions I have sketched here.

5.2 Political Moralities on a Map of Justice

The three dimensions and the six theories of justice as partly clashing interpretations of equality are presented schematically in Figure 1.[116] The dimensions are private vs. public control of property (or means of production), coupled with individual vs. mutual responsibility, local vs. global interests, and the identification of opportunities positionally vs. individualistically. The theories between

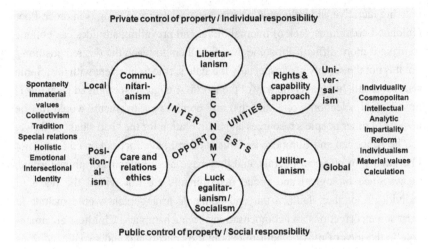

Figure 1 The map of justice as interpretations of equality

which the tensions are at their most intensive are (in the same order) libertar-ianism vs. luck egalitarianism and socialism, communitarianism vs. utilitarian-ism, and care and relations ethics vs. the rights and capabilities approach(es). The margins on the left and on the right list further juxtapositions between the local and positional vs. the global and universal views. These will enter my story later.

Before explaining the areas that I think the two principlisms occupy on the map, let me specify the descriptions of the ethics of care and the capabilities approach.

5.2.1 The Ethics of Care

While Kemp and partners in their report made rather vague references to the ethics of care, Beauchamp and Childress gave it a solid treatment already at the turn of the millennium. They briefly presented the work of Carol Gilligan and Annette Baier, noted Susan Sherwin's criticism, and stated the pros and cons of the theory from their own viewpoint.[117]

Gilligan challenged the view that rights, duties, contracts, and welfare calcu-lations represent the peak of moral development in young people. Studies in social psychology involving only boys and men had come to this conclusion, but when Gilligan included girls and women she discovered a new element. Female study subjects tended to emphasize values like compassion, fidelity, discernment, and love, and to give weight to special relationships of care, the mother-child relationship being the paradigm. This would seem to suggest that moral development in humans does not necessarily stop at liberal, consequentialist, or deontological stances, but can progress further to a more intimate and interpersonal ethos.[118]

Although Gilligan argued that men are inclined to look for voluntary associations and agreements while women lean on contextually given relationships, she did not claim that the distinction would be essentially gender-specific. It is just that, according to her, there are two main types of moral thinking, the ethics of care and the ethics of rights and justice, and women are more likely to assume the former – to care for and take care of others rather than make up quasilegal concepts to justify their actions.[119] Note that I have included the ethics of care in the map of justice at my own peril. According to its chief advocate, the creed stands in opposition to considerations of justice. However, since I see no reason to limit the use of the word to rights and contracts, as she does, I will take the risk.

Baier applied Gilligan's psychological observation more specifically to traditional moral theories. She saw these as one-sided and noted that they regularly promote impersonal, universal rules and rely on autonomous choices made by detached, free, and equal agents. Since human relationships are most often intimate, unchosen, and unequal, the prescriptions produced by such theories are frequently inadequate. Baier does not reject, outright, obligations arising from standard philosophical considerations, but points out that they cannot be all there is to morality. Concepts such as loving, caring, trusting, and bonding should also be taken into account in theories of ethics and their applications to real life.[120]

Although the ethics of care has natural links with feminism, it has also been criticized by feminist thinkers. Sherwin's argument is that celebrating gender- or biological-sex-related dispositions and character traits may be unwise in a fundamentally sexist culture. If women's disproportionate role in care work is a by-product of a patriarchal hegemony, embracing it as the true feminine morality could stand in the way of equality and commit women even more deeply to their subservient status. The role of care merits investigation, but rights and justice are still needed, for instance, to address gender imbalances in medicine, healthcare, and social work.[121]

Beauchamp and Childress agree with Sherwin that impartial principles have their place in bioethics. They point out, however, several areas in which considerations of care would be valuable and warn against confining such considerations to nursing and other areas that attract predominantly women.[122]

5.2.2 The Capabilities Approach

The ethics of care is contrasted on my map of justice with the capabilities approach as formulated by Martha Nussbaum. The main demarcation line is that

one is positional and the other universal. Care ethics assigns duties and opportunities on the basis of relationships and natural group memberships, while the
capabilities approach assigns them on the basis of contextual individuality.
People's positive, supported freedoms to achieve important goals were alluded
to in Kemp and his group's talk of capacity but not explained in detail by them.
Beauchamp and Childress did not highlight capabilities in their 2001 version,
but in the 2019 edition of *Principles of Biomedical Ethics* it has found its proper
place between egalitarianism, communitarianism, and well-being-focused
theories.[123]

The approach as presented by Nussbaum revolves around her list of ten
central human capabilities. My narrative will involve comparable catalogs by
others, so here is hers in the words of Beauchamp and Childress:[124]

1. *Life.* Being able to live a normal life without dying prematurely or existing
   in a reduced state making life not worth living
2. *Bodily health.* Being able to have good health, nutrition, and shelter
3. *Bodily integrity.* Being able to move freely, to be secure against violence,
   and to have opportunities for sexual satisfaction and reproductive choice
4. *Senses, imagination, and thought.* Being able to use these capacities in an
   informed and human way aided by an adequate and diverse education and
   in a context of freedom of expression
5. *Emotions.* Being able to have emotional attachments to persons and things
   so that one can love, grieve, and feel gratitude without having one's
   emotional development blunted by fear, anxiety, and the like
6. *Practical reason.* Being able to form a conception of the good and to
   critically reflect in planning one's life
7. *Affiliation.* Being able to live meaningfully in the company of others, with
   self-respect and without undue humiliation
8. *Other species.* Being able to live with concern for animals, plants, and
   nature generally
9. *Play.* Being able to play and enjoy recreational activities
10. *Control over one's environment.* Being able to participate as an active
    citizen in political choices pertaining to one's life and property.

Each of these ten capabilities forms the basis of a corresponding right. For social
justice to prevail, every human being must be equipped with every one of them at
least at a threshold level that secures the individual's dignity. Developing them
further to promote human flourishing would also be a worthy goal. Nonhuman
animals should not be coercively denied these capabilities, either.

Beauchamp and Childress comment that the resulting view is "extremely
demanding, perhaps as bold and ambitious as any theory of justice ever

devised."[125] The fair equality of opportunity suggested by Rawls that they saw as the limit in 2001 has, then, been replaced in 2019 by Nussbaum's account. Since both address opportunities and want to secure a wide range of them for all, the continuum is obvious.

5.2.3 Capitalism as a Shared Premise

The approximate positions of the American and European principlisms are marked in Figure 2 with three shapes: a quadrilateral on the right for exclusively American, another one on the left for exclusively European, and a triangle in the upper center for the ground they share. The approaches do not have to embrace all the interpretations of all the views that fall within their domain. There are further normative variables that are not visible in this two-dimensional portrait. A general agreement and the possibility of a palatable reading are enough. What the shapes exclude is at least equally important, though. If I have drawn the boundaries in the right places, the American and European principlisms should have difficulties in operating consistently outside their "own" areas on the map.

The American type of principlism can easily coexist with some forms of libertarianism, most aspects of the capabilities approach, and many liberal interpretations of communitarianism and utilitarianism. Beauchamp and Childress recognize libertarianism's relative coldness toward those in need but do not denounce the whole theory for it. They acknowledge the validity of community concerns, although the deeper nationalist and collectivist agendas are ruled out by their commitment to individualism. They have their doubts about extending healthcare entitlements as far as Nussbaum's capabilities,

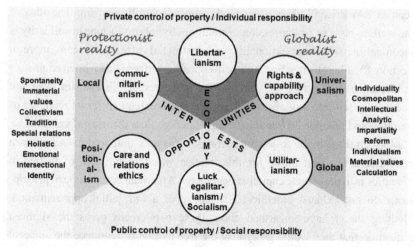

Figure 2 The American and European principlisms on a map of justice

utilitarian maximization, and Rawls's fair equality of opportunity, but do not deny the usefulness of these aspects in a more moderate application of their principles.

The excluded areas for American principlism are strict libertarianism, stringent utilitarianism, and any collectivist and holistic forms of communitarian and care ethics. The principles of autonomy, beneficence, nonmaleficence, and justice seem to support at least a decent minimum of publicly funded healthcare for all, maybe more, but definitely not everything for everybody. Care would seem to enter the model in that it is recognized as useful by Beauchamp and Childress in their account of Gilligan's and Baier's views. I submit, however, that while care in some everyday sense is a part of all healthcare, the more philosophical idea of an ethics based on special relations and interactions within them is not compatible with the specific impartiality and individualism of the American model.

The European type of principlism can coexist with most forms of communitarianism and with some elements of care ethics, capability ethics, and libertarianism. Kemp and partners seem to use a delicate from-local-to-almost-universal approach which fills the gap between Europe-centered community thinking and UN-type human rights. According to one, duties and entitlements are based on tradition; according to the other, universal human rights are based on European tradition. Unlike Beauchamp and Childress, who cherish the idea of worldwide, neutral universality, Kemp and his colleagues do not seem to mind this parochialism for the good of humanity.

The excluded areas for European principlism are care ethics when it becomes intersectional radicalism (more on this in Section 8), capability thinking when it is too individual-oriented, liberalism and libertarianism inasmuch as they are seen as "American" phenomena, and, especially, utilitarianism. The idea of the welfare state as an expression of traditionally inborn European solidarity is incompatible with intersectionality's reconstructed difference (again, more in Section 8), liberalism's free and self-choosing citizens, and libertarianism's indifference in the face of vulnerability and need. Utilitarianism does not necessarily fall into any of those traps, but it is condemned for its rejection of tradition and reliance on hedonism and related godless theories of value.[126]

More on these in the following sections – it is now time to draw my interim conclusion. My first thesis for this treatise was that the role of justice in bioethics is to perpetuate capitalist hegemony. American and European principlisms do not exhaust bioethics, but they give a fair initial approximation. Nothing that I have unearthed about these two creeds gives the slightest indication that they would go against the free market or renounce the adjacent global economic system based on continuous material growth. Capitalism can be criticized when it is taken to its protectionist or globalizing extremes and clear wrongdoing occurs, but the phenomenon in and of itself is not questioned. This is what it means to be in a hegemonic position – to be unquestioned. Insofar as American and European principlisms are concerned, then, the role of justice in bioethics is indeed to perpetuate capitalist hegemony.

6 Against Capitalism

6.1 Social Justice

Many bioethicists are likely to object, at this point, that equality, justice, and solidarity have roles in the discipline and its practical applications that are not aimed at "perpetuating capitalist hegemony." Increasing social justice in medicine, healthcare, and biomedical research is one such role. Scarce resources must be allocated, burdens and benefits need to be distributed, and priorities have to be set. Considerations of justice play an important part in making these decisions fair and equitable. Rosamond Rhodes, Margaret Battin, Anita Silvers, and their coauthors embody this line of thinking in their 2002 collection *Medicine and Social Justice: Essays on the Distribution of Health Care.*[127]

This objection is terminologically valid. Bioethicists from all corners of my map in Figures 1 and 2 try to ensure that distributive justice is done. They criticize choices that ignore vulnerable groups or the worst off. They attack practices and policies that harm rather than benefit populations or unduly restrict the liberty of individuals or groups. They shun solutions that are insensitive to prevailing values or discriminate against minorities. They reject arrangements that abandon people in need citing their own contribution to acquiring the need.

All these can become condemnations of the workings of capitalism. The vulnerable or the worst off can be ignored to maximize profits. Populations can be harmed and freedoms curtailed for the sake of economy. Attacks against values and violations of minority rights may be dictated by business reasons. If any of these is the case, the bioethicists raising the arguments are pointing out weaknesses in the capitalist system and suggesting restrictions on it.

Several considerations dilute, however, the force of this rebellion. One question mark is that different academics use different arguments in the debate, and these are not always mutually compatible. Beyond a bare minimum on which, say, Beauchamp and Childress could agree with Kemp and his group, the critical voices start canceling each other out. Defenders of the vulnerable clash with champions of the worst-off, harm-benefit optimizers with guardians of liberty, custodians of tradition with protectors of non-traditional minorities, and so on. All the views can claim universal or local validity, so the exclusively right response may be among them, but while the bickering continues, the wheels of capitalism keep turning. The doctrines supported by the American and European principlisms can also forge coalitions over seemingly unbridgeable ideological gaps and thereby increase the conceptual confusion and hence their indirect contribution to the status quo.

What is more, the wheels of capitalism would keep turning even if one of the views were proven to be overridingly superior. All the doctrines, even libertarianism, put some brakes on what are seen as excesses in global technological and business advances, but none of them halts the machine. Perhaps this is as it should be. Perhaps the machine does not need halting, only proper adjustments. I do, however, have in mind some reasons that would suggest otherwise.

6.2 Global Justice

At the turn of the millennium, bioethics was in a sense proceeding from its initial phase to the next one.[128] The first stage had been dominated by the liberation of patients and healthcare customers from the paternalism of medical professionals. The second stage added to the agenda the empowerment (or reempowerment) of professionals in care, research, and related fields.

On the technology and innovation side, a popular way of securing researchers more control over their work was to harmonize laws. To give an example, the research question of an international project on biobanks that I was involved in during the early 2000s was not, "Should human genetic databases be allowed?" but rather, "How can we make the regulation of human genetic databases consistent across national borders?"[129] This is a fine specimen of reflections on justice in bioethics and biolaw feeding directly into the smoother operation of the free-market, or capitalist, economy.

Healthcare professionals were empowered worldwide by a stronger ethics governance that was disseminated to all continents by the spread of the discipline and by international declarations.[130] The moral thinking behind these developments was and is, however, so obviously "Western" and "Global Northern" that questions began to arise about its wider applicability.[131] Detailed philosophical discussions on the universality or not of Beauchamp and Childress's principles are still ongoing.[132] Many bioethicists in the United States believe that the model, with proper checks and balances, works all over the world – as evidenced by the upbeat tone of Ronald Green, Aine Donovan, Steven Jauss, and their coauthors in the 2008 collection *Global Bioethics*.[133] Others, particularly ethicists in the Global South, have been less enthusiastic.[134]

In their contributions to global ethics, Heather Widdows, Donna Dickenson, and Sirkku Hellsten assumed a cautious view toward principlism and its allegedly universal reach. They advocated, however, cosmopolitan views and thought that justice, individual and communal, is pivotal and useful to world-wide bioethics, as long as the general and the particular can be adequately balanced.[135] Academics from Latin America,[136] Asia,[137] and Africa[138] called for approaches that would be culturally more sensitive and include issues like poverty, vulnerability, diversity, family ties, and local and regional traditions.

With global ethics, we move on to a new and challenging context. Some bioethical considerations can, in theory, be transferred to the novel setting. We can think about, say, research protocols in poor countries and regions, or the prevention of debilitating and lethal diseases, but as far as justice is concerned, the discussion is stuck between the different readings of equality as presented in Figures 1 and 2.

In research arrangements, should we respect, in a communitarian fashion, the authority of traditional local leaders? Or should we, with our capabilities hat on, defy them as oppressors of their people, and especially of women and minorities?[139] What we see as global justice depends on the answers to these questions.

As for diseases leading to disability and death, Simo Vehmas and I have used river blindness as an example.[140] In our study of this widely endemic disease with millions of victims in Third World countries, we noted that libertarianism is the only theory that cannot even in principle support international aid; recognized the corporate-social-responsibility angle, in that a supranational pharmaceutical company has made medication freely available to aid organizations since 1988; and observed that all other doctrines of justice could, with convenient interpretations, support global relief.[141] Despite the goodwill and caring in theory, though, nothing decisive has happened in the struggle against the malady, possibly because parochial or protectionist readings of equality are easier to adopt than universal and cosmopolitan ones.

These examples of global bioethics are representative and reveal two further aspects. The first is that in many cases we expect capitalism, here the pharma industry, to do what needs to be done – arrange sensitive consent procurement, agree to benefit sharing, produce a vaccine for river blindness, invent medications for other ailments, and generally make people's lives better. The second aspect is that the discussion tends to be confined to people. As Tuija Takala, among others, observed already in 2001, global ethics should also be about the environment – ecosystems, nonhuman animals, biodiversity, and the state of lands, oceans, seas, and the atmosphere.[142] These are seldom considered in analyses of biomedical research or international healthcare and infrastructure provision. River blindness actually offers a good example to the contrary. Apart from medication, one remedy that has made a difference has been the use of larvicides to reduce black fly populations in fast-flowing rivers.[143] The environmental impact of this chemical attack on nature has not always been fully assessed.

6.3 Capitalism, Growth, and Limits

My narrative is proceeding in a few interesting directions now. Justice in its social and global senses is employed to make people's lives better. Equality in its equal-shares-for-everyone meaning is not fully promoted anywhere, nor is it supported by most political moralities. In making people's lives better, considerations of justice rely on a relatively unrestricted market and thereby perpetuate capitalism, as stated in my first thesis. In addition to people, the environment should somehow be taken into account. If the current vocabularies cannot accommodate, even in theory, more extensive social-equality and ecological concerns, we may need new words, or new etymologies for existing ones. This is the point of my second thesis, namely that there is an imperative to reclaim moral and political concepts for resistance and emancipation.

Why, though, we might ask? Where is the fire? Contemplations of justice are in good use; fully equal shares are either an unattainable dream or a nightmare to be avoided; people are more important than the natural environment; and capitalism, while not perfect, is the only functioning economic system that we have.

On the last item (I will return to the other points in Section 7), we have already seen how Beauchamp and Childress as well as Kemp and his partners stay close to market thinking. In a 2021 interview, Peter Singer, too, confessed his reluctant alliance with capitalism.[144] The reporter suggested that in an early book on Marxism he had steered clear of communism, and certainly not advocated it as a way of living. Singer responded:

> That's true. I guess it's one way in which we ought not to live. And that is still relevant because, very often, when I speak about global poverty, somebody gets up and says, "Well, isn't the problem really capitalism? And shouldn't we be doing what we can do to overthrow capitalism?"[145]

Interested in this, the reporter pressed on and remarked that with Singer's advocacy of effective altruism (that you should earn billions to benefit charities with them) "the movement that has grown up around your work has ended up being very compatible with capitalism" – "for capitalism to almost be incorporated into your philosophical work." Singer denied the allegation, but did not denounce capitalism:

> I don't think capitalism is incorporated into my philosophical work. I think my philosophical work is neutral about what is the best economic system – but it's

also realistic, and I think we're stuck with capitalism for the foreseeable future. We are going to continue to have billionaires, and it's much better that we have billionaires like Bill and Melinda Gates or Warren Buffett, who give away most of their fortune thoughtfully and in ways that are highly effective, than billionaires who just build themselves bigger and bigger yachts.[146]

The argument is, then, that while capitalism has its shortcomings, it is inescapable, and we can only hope for good capitalists and cheer them on when they are in evidence.

A similar reliance on a more humane capitalism has been detectable in Martha Nussbaum's capabilities approach[147] and Carol Gilligan's ethics of care.[148] Both seem to believe that once the full potential of women is released from patriarchal oppression, the profit- and growth-oriented market economy will deliver more equitable outcomes. Both Nussbaum and Gilligan are essentially liberal thinkers, so this is par for the course for them. More straightforward and profound criticisms of capitalism could be expected from feminist philosophers who are amenable to, say, Shulamith Firestone's 1970 take *The Dialectic of Sex: The Case for a Feminist Revolution*[149] or Mary Mahowald's ideas on Marxist medical ethics.[150] But more on their kind of thinking later (Section 8).

In the meantime, my suggested objection to free-market growth is simpler.

Capitalism is an economic and political system that makes some people happy and others unhappy. The doctrine of classical liberalism taught that the system's driving force is growth. When populations and economies grow, more and more people will be happy, maybe at some point even the majority.[151] Karl Marx and Friedrich Engels believed that capitalism is such a strong force that its growth will make everyone happy, in a consumerist kind of way, before it meets the limits of technology and nature. After this, the only resource to exploit is the workforce. It will be exploited because the system cannot survive without perpetual growth, and alienation, class struggle, and revolution will ensue.[152]

Time ran out on Marx and Engels's prediction, however, as capitalism met other, environmental boundaries. An early warning was given by the Great Horse Manure Crisis of London. In 1894, *The Times* announced that since horse droppings can be carted out of big cities only by horses, producing more droppings, "in 50 years, every street in London will be buried under nine feet of manure."[153] While this threat was averted by the invention and use of motorcars, gasoline, and oil, the solution brought us, in time, something even more alarming, namely climate change. And although some say that sustainable development will be a remedy to this, it is more than feasible that it is not, and that some people, even some currently happy ones, will be left in or thrown into the ranks of the unhappy.

The point of this simplified story is to serve as a reminder of an apparent circle in humanity's current tactic in encountering challenges. Technology and business, under the auspices of corporate and state capitalism, create crises, the crises are solved by technology and business, under the auspices of corporate and state capitalism, and more crises are produced. This would not be fatal if material growth could go on forever. We could just stumble from crisis to crisis like humankind has done before. It is different this time, though, or so we are led to believe. With climate change, loss of biodiversity, and a plethora of other social and environmental issues, it seems that growth cannot go on forever, after all. There are planetary limits that the international community recognizes and has vowed to respect. Since bioethics cannot avoid this issue any more than other disciplines trying to resolve issues of justice, a short detour to growth, sustainability, and sustainable development, as Maarit Laihonen and I, among many others, have investigated them, is in order.[154]

7 Growth, Sustainability, and Sustainable Development

7.1 From Management to Conservation

We have, then, two potentially contradictory beliefs. Capitalism must go on because it is the only economic system that we have, but it cannot go on because it requires continuous growth, and growth has limits that we are rapidly reaching. The current attempt to deal with this is by modifying the second belief. Capitalism must continue, but since it will in its present form crash into planetary limits, with dire consequences to humanity and the environment, it has to continue in a different form. This different form is now known as sustainable development.[155] It is a UN-driven project and has close links with global bioethics and its endeavor to promote justice by internationally recognized goals and rights. Let us see how this approach came into being and why it will probably not solve our problems. This will strengthen the case for my second thesis, that a more profound change is needed.

Sustainable development as a UN concept is a unique combination of the preexisting ideas of managing and conserving natural resources. These have a history that explains some of the features of today's international policies.

In the eighteenth century, concerns about deforestation and scarcity of timber incited the public authorities, first in Germany and then in other countries, to start treating forests systematically as measurable resources. The thinking was that woodlands need proper scientific attention to yield better crops over longer periods of time.[156] The temporal aspect is at the core of sustainability. The managed entity should be sustained, made to last longer than just now, in many cases even to be available to future generations. Scientific forestry that promotes the use of land and forests in this way sounds, at least initially, like a reasonable idea. What could be wrong with making wise use of perishable resources?

The entity to be sustained can be chosen and defined in different ways, though, depending on the motivation. For scientific forestry in the eighteenth and nineteenth centuries, the entity was the quality and quantity of timber, and the motivation was economico-political. Governments wanted to take better care of the state's assets, which was well within their remit. This meant, however, the eviction of the general public from their traditional gathering and hunting grounds and nonhuman animals and plants from their natural habitats. The volume of wood production was increased, but the rights and well-being of ordinary citizens were ignored, constrained, and reduced, as were the living conditions of nonhuman species.[157]

Fast-forward a couple of centuries, and conservation for more ecological and equitable ends had come to challenge the management approach exemplified by scientific forestry. After the Second World War, the notions that would become the core of environmental sustainability started to rise within different scientific fields and civil society. These notions were based on a perceived conflict between dwindling natural resources and an ever-growing human population, aggravated by ecological degradation. A Malthusian revival was instigated and fueled by three best-sellers: Fairfield Osborn's *Our Plundered Planet*,[158] William Vogt's *Road to Survival*,[159] and Paul (and Anne, whose name was omitted at the publisher's insistence) Ehrlich's *The Population Bomb*.[160] The authors argued that the natural environment had been systematically polluted and corrupted, partly beyond redemption, and that this would soon have disastrous economic and social consequences. Since resources cannot be sufficiently increased, they continued, the only way to prevent further calamities is population control.[161]

The idea of restricting the number of people on the planet as a moral imperative was for decades a part of the prevailing political ethos in many circles. Birth control fitted, for different reasons, the agendas of several otherwise quarreling parties of the time. Those who believed in the healing power of eugenics, of producing a better human race, had lost their hope in encouraging good stock to breed and had resolved to discourage the bad stock from having children.[162] Neo-Malthusians like Osborn, Vogt, Ehrlich, and Ehrlich believed in Thomas Malthus, who had prophesied that, if uncurbed, human populations will always outgrow the availability of resources, leading to violence, famine, and misery. Feminists who wanted to secure women's control over their bodies saw family planning as a way of achieving this and therefore supported the use of contraceptives and other voluntary methods of reducing pregnancies.[163]

The Neo-Malthusians did not propose detailed policies for checking population sizes, and their critics, like Malthus's adversaries previously,[164] had a field day inventing what they saw as ethically dubious ways of reducing the number of people.[165] The whole idea of "fighting the population explosion" slowly drifted into relative oblivion, perhaps not least because China's one-child policy was seen as a moral failure and a tragic intrusion on family life and reproductive freedom due to the violent practices through which it was implemented. Aspects of Neo-Malthusianism seem to be alive in international declarations and agreements, however, as evidenced by the frequent use of such expressions as "growing population," "limited resources," and "land and ecosystem degradation."[166]

Malthusians have been challenged by Cornucopians – futurists and political theorists who believe either that a growing population is a resource rather than a threat; or that although a growing population could be a threat, the threat can be removed by technological advances; or that a just distribution of what the Earth can provide would guarantee well-being for all, regardless of the number of people.[167]

Insofar as Cornucopians put their faith in perpetual economic growth as the source of future plenitude, they have been under challenge since the 1960s. The first systematic predictions of the eventual depletion of Earth's resources were produced for the Club of Rome, a non-profit, nongovernmental organization founded in 1968 by a group of European businesspeople and scientists. *The Limits to Growth* and *Mankind at the Turning Point*[168] endeavored to show, by detailed computer simulations, that the planet's resources will be exhausted sooner or later unless we change our ways drastically. The 1973 oil crisis amplified the message, but not all critics were convinced by the reliability of the methodologies or the feasibility of the suggestions for changing our ways.[169]

Half a century later the Club of Rome was still on the same message.[170] Although some of the early predictions had turned out to be overly pessimistic, their fiftieth-anniversary report *Transformation Is Feasible* reiterated the main claims.[171] Corrective action is necessary, and neither maintaining a business-as-usual approach nor accelerating economic growth is a proper response. The authors argue that even if governments could address the issues of poverty, hunger, and inequalities in education (which they deem doubtful), environmental goals would still be missed by conventional policies. "There is high risk," they state, "for pushing the Earth's life supporting systems beyond irreversible trigger-points by 2050."[172] According to the report, we need to stop using fossil fuels, employ rigorous family planning, and level wealth inequalities considerably. Some of these policies would, of course, hurt fossil-dependent industries, offend those who abhor Neo-Malthusian antinatalism, and expand governmental control over economies, but this is apparently a price that the authors are willing to pay.

7.2 From Conservation to Sustainable Development Goals

Responding to the concerns of the Club of Rome and others, in 1972 the UN organized in Stockholm a conference on humanity's relationship and mutual dependency with the natural environment, but it soon became clear that more was needed to get the issues properly addressed.[173] The International Union for Conservation of Nature and Natural Resources (IUCN) made the first important move by inventing and introducing in 1980 a new concept, sustainable development.[174]

In their report *World Conservation Strategy: Living Resource Conservation for Sustainable Development*,[175] the IUCN observed how the management and conservation of natural resources are two different things, with different values and logics, and with a tangible potential to clash. Management practices that have purely or mainly economic aims can wreak havoc on the environment and thereby challenge conservation for ecological purposes. Since the ways in which this can happen are myriad and the chains and interrelations complex, the practices involved and their networks should be systematically and methodically analyzed and assessed. Only when these analyses and assessments have either enabled resolution of the conflict or exposed the value choices that have to be made can the resulting decisions contribute to economic progress that is also ecologically sound. This progress, if it is possible, can be called sustainable development.

The reading here presumes that even the best economic management, be it scientific forestry as per my earlier example or something else, can lead to ecologically detrimental consequences. This presumption was not universally shared in the 1980s. It was becoming evident that the industrialization of Third World countries added to the environmental decay that had already been started by more affluent nations. Many believed, however, that the real culprits were bad management, technological backwardness, and lack of modernization. The Bhopal gas tragedy in 1984 and the Chernobyl nuclear disaster in 1986 seemed to support this view. Doing too much of a good thing was not an idea that would have alarmed everyone. Besides, the Cold War and the threat of an impending nuclear holocaust distracted people's minds from more distant issues like atmospheric pollution and loss of species.

In 1983, the UN set up a group called the World Commission on Environment and Development and appointed Gro Harlem Brundtland, the Prime Minister of

Norway in 1981, 1986–9, and 1990–6, as its first chair. The task of the Commission was twofold. They were supposed to show how countries in the Global South could be helped to modernize their industries and political systems to make people's lives better. At the same time, they were supposed to make sure that the advances would not pose an environmental threat that would come back to haunt populations in the Global North.

The Brundtland Commission borrowed the term introduced by the IUCN and gave it a new appearance, encapsulated in their well-known definition:

> Sustainable development is development that meets the needs of the present without compromising the ability of future generations to meet their own needs.[176]

The language of this passage reveals the difference between the two interpretations. For the IUCN, it had been crucial to distinguish between economic progress and conservation, and to see to it that their conflicts are properly recognized and solved. For the Brundtland Commission, everything is one and all good things can be achieved simultaneously. According to them, well-managed economic development will also promote social equality and ecological aims. No conflict analyses or resolutions are needed.

The Commission's concise definition is open to different readings. Universally understood, they could be seen as saviors of the poor in Third World countries, champions of future generations, and defenders of good economic values. Alternatively, a lead politician of an emerging oil and gas power wanted to secure Norway's newfound wealth based on environmentally detrimental energy production and hinder ecological degradation elsewhere to safeguard the future of her grandchildren on a livable planet. Be that as it may, the Commission carved in stone the view, cherished by rising neoliberals the world over, that social and environmental issues need not be taken into account directly, as they can be tackled by good technology and business practices and governance.[177]

Several UN environmental and climate conferences interpreted and reinterpreted the Brundtland Commission's findings and especially their prescriptive implications. The starting point, as observed, was that there are three equally important dimensions to be considered – economic, social, and ecological – but that governing the first by the principles of sustainable development will help humanity achieve all three in one fell swoop. Meetings in Rio de Janeiro, Kyoto, and elsewhere refined the message until the 2015 summits in Paris and New York produced and released the current model – a list of seventeen Sustainable Development Goals (SDGs) and 169 specifications to them.

The SDGs are, put briefly: (1) end poverty, (2) end hunger, (3) ensure health and well-being for all, (4) ensure quality education for all, (5) achieve gender equality and empower all women and girls, (6) ensure water and sanitation for all, (7) ensure affordable and clean energy for all, (8) promote economic growth and decent work for all, (9) build infrastructure, promote industrialization, and foster innovation, (10) reduce inequality, (11) make human settlements inclusive and safe, (12) ensure sustainable production and consumption, (13) take action to combat climate change, (14) conserve oceans and seas, (15) protect terrestrial ecosystems and protect biodiversity, (16) promote peace and justice, and (17) strike global partnerships.[178]

All these goals, according to declaration language, are equal, all must be pursued at all times, and there can be no trade-offs. This is in line with current UN thinking about human rights. Apart from being universal, these are supposed to be indivisible – one goal or right must not be ignored or violated to pursue another.[179] I will return briefly to this ends-do-not-justify-means theme from another angle in my own suggestion (Section 9). In the meantime, the cognate case of a recent European bioeconomy strategy illustrates how the idea of indivisibility is applied to practice in real-life international policy. The following is based on my ongoing work with Johanna Ahola-Launonen, Sofi Kurki, Maarit Laihonen, Merja Porttikivi, Nicolas Balcom Raleigh, Amos Taylor, Liisa Saarenmaa, Tuija Takala, and Markku Wilenius.[180]

Bioeconomy is a good example of an endeavor to solve global environmental problems through technology and business innovations. At heart, it promises to replace the current depletable, greenhouse-gas-emitting fossil economy with the use of renewable, organic, clean biomasses. The European Union's (EU) 2018 bioeconomy strategy illustrates, however, how already on the level of declaration language the noble aims get transformed into a different kind of reality.

The strategy starts boldly by stating that we are challenged by limited resources, climate change, land and ecosystem degradation, a growing population, a need to achieve sustainability, and a need to ensure the future prosperity of EU citizens.[181] The initial formulation suggests that Europe and the world will be saved by a bioeconomy that adheres to the UN SDGs. As the document progresses, though, the motivating challenges take a back seat or disappear altogether. Saving the planet and its inhabitants becomes a secondary issue, while stress is laid on new ways of production and consumption, the modernization of industries, and investing in novel technologies and businesses. It is an economy strategy for a capitalist economic alliance, so no surprise there. When we placed the strategy on my map of political moralities, however, some interesting details, relevant also to the roles of justice in bioethics, came to light.[182] Figure 3 sketches the findings.

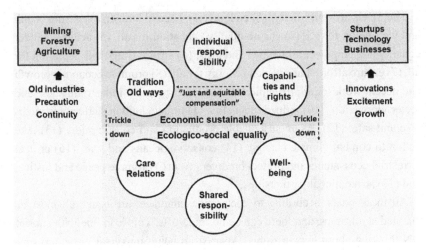

Figure 3 A sustainable development bioeconomy strategy on a map of justice

The strategy's motivating ideals belong to the lower half of the map: caring relations with nature (care ethics), the promotion of human and nonhuman well-being (utilitarianism), and our shared responsibility for these (luck egalitarianism and socialism). Its practical suggestions and implementation, on the other hand, are confined to the upper half of Figure 3: tradition and old ways (communitarianism), individual responsibility (libertarianism), and promotion of capabilities (capability approach).

The driving force of the EU strategy seems to be a version of the capability approach, and at its core is an insistence on making the world better by ability-creating innovations, excitement, and growth. When this attitude is combined with libertarian economic ideals, startups, new businesses, and technology development take pride of place. In theory, libertarians should not condone any state or international subsidies, but the situation here seems to be different, perhaps because old industries compete with the new, and public support will be available in any case.

Older industries are not forgotten in the implementation of the EU strategy, either. Although excessive forestry reduces biodiversity and coal mining and oil and gas rigging increase carbon emissions, they still enjoy the status of recognized if receding businesses. Their historical legitimacy as cornerstones of industrialization seems to entitle them to special compensations, both nationally and internationally.[183] It would not be just and equitable, their defenders say, if they were abruptly shut down, forcing their owners and workers to find new lines of work on their own.

Sustainability is always about sustaining something. The EU bioeconomy strategy exemplifies the current UN SDG thinking, which aims to perpetuate material growth. This can be called economic sustainability. The strategy's response to the remaining concerns of development and conservation, ecolo-gico-social equality or ecological and social sustainability, is indirect. Economic activities will create a trickle-down effect, whereby the wealth accumulated by new industries will increase the well-being of populations and guarantee the flourishing of the natural environment.

8 Three Kinds of Economically Sustainable Bioethics

8.1 Lists with Hidden Priorities

The EU bioeconomy strategy reflects the current UN ideology, and this leans on sustainable development as defined by the SDGs tactic. Wherever this kind of thinking is applied, it tends to produce lists of things to be achieved and things to be avoided. Bioethics is not an exception. Insofar as the discipline has endeavored to become socially relevant and internationally effective, it has moved closer to administration and law, and in these fields explicit and detailed instructions are convenient.

Three theories of justice are more amenable to the rules approach than the rest: libertarianism, the capabilities view, and communitarianism. Care ethics emphasizes lived experience over formalism, utilitarianism recognizes only one fundamental axiom, and socialism, at least in its critical forms, is more con-cerned about overturning existing regulations than creating new ones.

Libertarianism's list is short and leaves less room for interpretation than most others. People should not actively take each other's lives, inflict serious bodily harm on one another, or interfere with each other's freedom. They should not actively interfere with one another's belongings, either. And they should keep the contracts and agreements they freely make. The world is not entirely libertarian, however. Although it may be predominantly run by supranational corporations, nation-states and their coalitions still have a say in matters and, maybe, so do the civil societies in those nations, that is, individual citizens and their associations. Defenders of economic laissez-faire ally themselves, there-fore, with other forces. The choreography in the case of bioeconomy was sketched in Figure 3, and similar alliances exist in bioethics.

When libertarians and capability promoters join forces, they assume, on an international level, lists like the UN's seventeen SDGs or Martha Nussbaum's ten central capabilities. These two lists are quite compatible. Once we end poverty and hunger and ensure health and well-being for all, as decreed by SDGs 1–3, Nussbaum's points 1 and 2, life and bodily health, seem to be covered to a considerable extent. Securing quality education and gender equal-ity; empowering women and girls; ensuring water supply, sanitation, affordable energy, and decent work and living conditions for all; conserving the natural environment; and promoting peace and justice (SDGs 4–8, 10, 11, 13–16) would take us a long way toward fulfilling Nussbaum's requirements 4–10, on bodily integrity; senses, imagination, and thought; emotions; practical reason; affiliation; relationships with other species; play; and control over one's environment.

The SDGs that do not find a direct match in Nussbaum's central capabilities are (9) building infrastructure, promoting industrialization, and fostering innovation, (12) ensuring sustainable production and consumption, and (17) striking global partnerships. Nothing in Nussbaum's work prevents, however, recognizing all these as material and political instruments for supporting the more human-related aims. Moreover, none of Nussbaum's capabilities suggests reducing populations or downsizing the human footprint. It seems safe, then, to assume that economic growth is a fit with her thinking. Perpetuating capitalist hegemony in the sense that I have specified looms large. It is worth noting that economic growth is coupled with decent work for all in SDG 8, indicating that the drafters of the SDGs see the former as a necessary condition for the latter.

Nussbaum is not the only theorist who has thought that a list of central goods is desirable. John Finnis in his neo-Thomist (Aristotelian Roman Catholic natural law) theory had already suggested in 1980 that reason and morality require us to take into account and stress the values of life, knowledge, play, aesthetic experience, sociability (friendship), practical reasonableness, and religion.[184] The language is different at times, but the accounts are virtually identical. The fact that Nussbaum and Finnis share common ground[185] has not been widely recognized, possibly because they differ sharply in their political views.[186]

The place that Finnis's doctrine would occupy on my map of justice in Figures 1–3 depends on the reading. If the values that he holds are universal, as could be expected of a natural law theory, the capabilities corner would seem like the right position. If we think of Roman Catholicism as one religion among others, the positional communitarian corner could be better. Yet another possibility would be the idea suggested by Kemp and his partners for European principles: initially local but somehow becoming global through historical inevitability. In the middle case, being one among many, Finnis would have to explain why his list is better than the numerous rule books, implicit or explicit, that local communities can claim as their spontaneously grown and hence legitimate tradition.

Finnis does explain his "central case viewpoint" in a passage that is worth citing:

> Thus, the central case viewpoint itself is the viewpoint of those who not only appeal to practical reasonableness but also are practically reasonable, that is

to say: consistent; attentive to all aspects of human opportunity and flourishing, and aware of their limited commensurability; concerned to remedy
deficiencies and breakdowns, and aware of their roots in the various aspects
of human personality and in the economic and other material conditions of
social interaction.[187]

Although this is a jurisprudential position, it illustrates a choice that all those
rooting for lists of good and bad things have to make, including in bioethics.
What to do in situations in which values are in conflict? Should we name one
main goal, as the EU bioeconomy strategy explicitly does? Or should we hang
on to the pluralism and then let a "practically reasonable" person decide? Will
that person say that we should stop material growth? Not in the standard
readings of communitarianism, libertarianism, and the capability approach in
bioethics. So, are there other alternatives?

8.2 Eugenic Liberal and Social Democracy

Communitarianism and utilitarianism are for most intents and purposes incompatible. Their contradictory background assumptions are sketched in the margins of Figures 1 and 2. Communitarians support spontaneously shaped
practices, immaterial values, collectivism, and respect for tradition as well as
traditionally formed relations and identities. Utilitarians want to scrutinize all
these in the light of the well-being of as many as possible. Some practices,
traditions, values, group feelings, and forms of respect may survive the test, but
not all of them do, and when they do not, utilitarians have to reject them. And
even when they do condone an organically grown practice, they do it, from the
communitarian viewpoint, on faulty grounds. For the latter, the justification of
a custom is in its being a recognized custom, not in its ability to produce
measurable well-being.

Neither of the two views is immune to considerations of interests, though,
and where interests coincide, pragmatic agreement is possible. This has
already been in evidence twice in my narrative. Antifeminists, racists, eugenicists, and medical doctors fought side by side to ban abortions in the nineteenth century, and in the mid-twentieth century eugenicists, Malthusian
conservationists, and feminists found common ground in their support of
birth control. These were both matters of human reproduction, and this is
also the area in which nationalist communitarians and aggregative utilitarians
could see, and have seen, eye to eye. Since the political product of the
combination can be a kind of social democracy (which in the United States
is likened to socialism), this could be seen as a potential challenger for at least
some forms of capitalism.

The currently popular version of a eugenic society is liberal democratic. As argued by Buchanan, Brock, Daniels, Wikler, and others,[188] the state can allow parents to select the genetically most desired offspring, or not, as they wish, and to use prevailing opportunities to enhance their children's abilities biologically and biochemically, or not, as they wish. This would be good for individuals who come into being in that they would not have to suffer from preventable ailments. It would leave parents free to decide their progeny's initial and essential characteristics and chances in life. And it would serve justice by eliminating inequalities both prenatally and when the children are already in existence.

Objections to this kind of thinking abound.[189] It is unnatural and dangerous to play God with children's lives like this.[190] The children can be harmed by the technologies. Allowing the choice would be unjust because it would give an edge to those whose parents can afford the expensive procedures. Selecting able-bodied and healthy children would discriminate against the disabled and the ill. It would also send a message saying that people with disabilities should not live. A false sense of control and individualism would weaken solidarity and community feeling. A Brave New World would ensue. The world as we know it would come to an end.

I have sieved the arguments for and against liberal eugenics before[191] and will not repeat the exercise here. Suffice it to say that neither its proponents nor its opponents pose a threat to capitalism and continuous material growth. The opponents in the communitarian camp make sure that this is not the alliance with utilitarianism that I promised, either. For that, we need to go back in history, first about a century and then one or two more.[192]

In the 1930s, many intellectuals and politicians in Sweden (and in other countries) wanted to establish a socially conscious and democratic welfare state, where all citizens could enjoy equal security. They argued that such a modern social-democratic welfare state is possible, but only if everyone's contribution is adequate. Natural and social sciences can guide the pursuit of human well-being regardless of biological, ethnic, and cultural differences. Idleness, stupidity, and crime, however, cannot be tolerated, because they would corrode the foundation of the rationally organized society. People who do not work, or who cannot be assigned to jobs that require mental alertness, do not advance the national product, and criminals deliberately drain common resources. Since individuals like these are a burden to a just society, it would be an advantage if they could be detected at an early stage, preferably before they are even born.[193]

This is where Swedish social democrats thought that eugenics could help them. If scientists could identify individuals whose children would probably be a burden to others, the information could be used to prevent the existence of unproductive citizens and the emergence of socially unnecessary needs. Eugenicists in Sweden went on to sterilize tens of thousands of people, who were suspected to bear, given the opportunity, progeny which would be genetically unfit to the welfare state. In addition to the mentally and physically deficient, they targeted a relatively small, itinerant Tattare population, who were believed to be racially different from the rest of the "Nordic" Swedes.[194]

So, here we have an example of a social order which is aggregately (and collectively) utilitarian, not exactly liberal, and has possibly redeeming factors in the eyes of nationalist communitarians. To justify the nationalist association, we would have to go further back in history, to the challenge that Romanticism posed against Enlightenment thinking in the eighteenth and nineteenth centuries.

The industrial revolution of the time led to the creation of an urban proletariat, among whom a plethora of social and health problems could be detected. One explanation was that when the noble savages of the countryside were ripped from their rural roots and transferred into cities, they lost their natural dignity and started to degenerate. At the bottom of this phenomenon was the idea, innocuous enough, that people, like all living beings, flourish best on their home soil.[195]

With a little assistance from Darwinian biology, however, nationalism, racism, and xenophobia formed, and can still form, a genocidal mix that we would not like to see put into practice anymore.[196] Establishing a palatable national social democracy seems, then, to be conceptually and ethically out of our reach, although some countries with strong populist minorities appear to disagree with this. Fortunately, the problem does not fall within my remit here. Although social democracy as an economic arrangement can be seen as "socialist" from a libertarian or neoliberal viewpoint, it was in the 1930s Sweden and it is in today's Scandinavian countries deeply rooted in continuous material growth. Although the freedom of the market was and is curbed to provide social security, capitalism is the unquestioned foundation of the economy, local and global.

8.3 The Feminist Alternative and Human Rights

Critical and liberal feminist bioethics occupy an interesting stretch on my map of justice. Figure 4 presents this (the ascending rectangle) and the last section's eugenics alternative (descending).

Feminist ethics can, in theory, be found anywhere on the map, so other locations and alliances are possible. They are not, however, widely embraced in today's feminist bioethics.

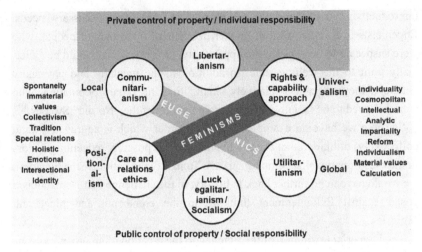

Figure 4 The eugenic and feminist alliances on a map of justice

Catharine Beecher and Harriet Stowe held in the nineteenth century that women are the moral backbone of societies, managing households, safeguarding the virtues of their family members, and taking on a Christ-like role of self-denying benevolence.[197] Elizabeth Cady Stanton agreed that women do tend to sacrifice themselves for their families, but she also argued that two further advances would be beneficial: women should exercise their virtues in the public sphere, as well, *and* they should attend to their own self-development.[198] At least partial agreement with communitarianism is possible in these cases.[199]

Harriet Taylor Mill and John Stuart Mill argued, also in the nineteenth century, that women are in many fields of life as capable as men and should therefore be given an equal chance to enter them. There may be professions or tasks that are not in the end suited for most female aspirants, but even in those cases artificial restrictions are unnecessary. If people belonging to a distinct group do not seem to make it in a given occupation, they will probably stop pursuing it. The freedom to try is, however, important, lest we miss the best workers for some jobs due to irrational customs.[200] Utilitarian considerations meet here feminist ones.

Twentieth-century feminism did not center on women's traditional roles, nor did it seek support from utilitarianism. Firestone's radical Freudo-Marxism was closer to the mainstream at the time bioethics was born. Interestingly, however, individualist or libertarian feminists from the diametrically opposed camp wanted to reclaim the beginnings of women's liberation. Sharon Presley and Joan Kennedy Taylor, among others, argued that the first feminist activists were individualists and libertarians,[201] a claim supported partly by Mill and Mill's views. Libertarian feminists wanted, and want, the law to treat women and men alike, without discrimination either way.

This assumption of sameness, or its criticism, is the root of critical feminist bioethics, as it emerged during the last decades of the twentieth century. Rosemary Tong and Nancy Williams have, following Eva Feder Kittay, usefully divided the criticism into three categories: "(1) the difference approach, (2) the dominance approach, and (3) the diversity approach."[202] According to the first, women and men are different and have different roles in society. If women became like men, there would be no altruistic caregivers and life would be considerably harsher. According to the second, the gender-based, culturally enforced position of caregivers subordinates women to men. We must identify and expose structures that keep this up, in the hope that awareness leads to liberation and equality. According to the third, discrimination does not stop at the female–male line. In addition to the women–men situation that has to be dealt with, work must also go on in more intersectional directions. What are the combinations of biologically, psychologically, socially, and politically con-structed characteristics that prevent equality?

Kittay singles out dependency workers – women who take care of other people but who are not adequately recognized and compensated for their work.[203] For genuine equality to prevail, we should provide these women, whether their labor takes place in the public or in the private domain, with the material, social, and political equality that is currently not within their reach. At the turn of the millennium, this suggestion had considerable impact on the development of feminist bioethics and prompted academics to point out many new groups that can be defined either by their dependency or by their depend-ency work. During the last two decades, though, the focus in bioethics has shifted from care laborers to the subjects of care, a trend that started immedi-ately after Kittay's revelation.[204]

One of the upshots of the shift has been that feminist studies have diversified and metamorphized into gender, disability, postcolonial, and difference studies, with an emphasis on lesbian, gay, bisexual, transgender, and queer (LGBTQ) concerns. Another effect of the shift has been that individual recipients of special attention have returned to the limelight, albeit that they are now increasingly defined by their intersectionality. This is how a person's capabilities, and human rights, have become associated with the ethics of relations and care, forging an alliance (the ascending rectangle in Figure 4) which clearly works in practice but defies logic by bringing together positional and universal views of equality and justice.

In 2022 Alison Jaggar defended human rights against the capability theory and against the main objections to the rights approach in feminist ethics.[205] These are Jaggar's reasons for rejecting Nussbaum's conception:

She contends that this conception articulates a cross-cultural and trans-historical consensus on the central and basic human functions, reflecting "the actual self-interpretations and self-evaluations of human beings in history" (Nussbaum 1995: 72–75). However, Nussbaum offers little evidence that her list of capabilities indeed reflects a tacit universal consensus and her writings quickly dismiss disagreements; she advocates "participatory dialogue" about how postulated capabilities might be specified locally but not about which capabilities reach the list or whether list-making is the best approach. My own view is that any ethical vision guiding global development must emerge from extensive and explicit democratic discussion that addresses means along with ends. For this reason, I believe that human rights, properly construed, have better credentials than capabilities as a universal standard of development.[206]

Since human rights, too, form a list, the main objection here must be that Nussbaum's central capabilities appear to have an ivory-tower origin, which makes them less credible than negotiated, internationally agreed entitlements.

Jaggar goes on to observe some main feminist objections to confidence in legal rights.[207] They can be used to strengthen men's power over women, as in privacy legitimizing domestic violence and freedom of expression justifying misogynist pornography. The formal equality of rights may have different outcomes for unequals, as in no-fault divorce committing women but not men to poverty. Special rights combating inequalities lead to women being seen as vulnerable and possibly as less reliable workers. Rights enable women to harm themselves, as seen in the cases of excessive cosmetic surgery and prostitution.

These are all formidable charges against human rights as they are currently conceptualized and implemented. Jaggar believes, however, that adjustments to legal interpretations can remedy the situation and enable the rights apparatus to promote genuine equality. The key to this, according to her, would be to proceed "by imagining the normative human as female rather than male."[208] This would, she argues, change for the better the way we understand the implicit normative force of words like "we," "our," and "ordinary language." It would also move us away from mere logical analyses of the language of morality and justice and make us more sensitive to metaphors, symbols, and nonlogical implications such as emphases, silences, and omissions.[209] An ethic built around this vision, Jaggar suggests, would produce an overlapping consensus among feminist thinkers.[210]

9 The Is, the Should, and the Can

9.1 The Is and the Should of Roles of Justice in Bioethics

What the roles of justice in bioethics are and what they should be have now been charted. Bioethics emerged in the United States in the 1960s and 1970s and took its early influences from millennia of medical and healthcare ethics and from social and political movements. In the American and then European principlist models it assigned justice the role of devising rules for nondiscrimination in research and prioritization and redistribution in the provision of healthcare. Theories of justice as partly clashing interpretations of equality offered, and offer, more precise suggestions for nondiscrimination, prioritization, and redistribution, and the principlist models agree with different sets of them. In agreeing with the theories of justice, the principlist models favor libertarian, communitarian, and capability approaches, paying some lip service to luck egalitarian and socialist, care and relations, and utilitarian ideals. The overall picture is that capitalism, or the economic ideology of continuous material growth, is not questioned by any of the views on which bioethics as an academic-professional discipline is based.

More political attempts at social and global justice have challenged the excesses of capitalism but stayed within its confines. A contemporary example at the time of writing this illustrates the matter. The coronavirus disease 2019 (COVID-19) pandemic has raised, among other things, issues about the order in which citizens in more affluent countries should be vaccinated and the perceived injustice of less affluent countries having to wait their turn until the situation is under control in the Global North. Worthy considerations, but where do we look for answers? In the supranational pharmaceutical industry, of course. How to make more and quicker? Should we tweak the patenting system for these situations? Should the process be spearheaded by corporate or state capitalism?

Yet the problem we all recognize, if international agreements and declarations are a measure, is that material growth cannot go on forever. Climate change and environmental degradation have set in motion processes that we need to check before planetary boundaries are reached, biodiversity gone, and nutrition and clean water the privilege of just a few. Unless we do, people cannot live decent lives, nonhuman animals suffer, and nature is irretrievably damaged. Halting these processes is the basis of sustainability thinking, and sustainability thinking, again if international official consensus is to be trusted, should inform everything that we do, including bioethics.

It is not, however, enough that we recognize the problem, if we are not willing to tackle it appropriately. As seen in the case of the European bioeconomy strategy, solutions are being sought from practices that caused the problems in the first place. The combination of libertarian, capability, and communitarian thinking produces momentary economic sustainability, that is, innovations, further material growth, compensations for older industries, and the hope of a trickle-down phenomenon that will promote ecologico-social equality as a side effect. The likeliest result is that ecological and social questions will remain unanswered.

In ethics and bioethics, the combination has so far produced lists of good things: Nussbaum's capabilities, Finnis's goods dictated by practical reasonableness, the American and European principles, and catalogs of human rights – sparse for libertarians and more extensive for the UN. In all these cases, the authors of the lists assure that all values will be accounted for equally. This idea of indivisibility can be developed in two directions. We can claim that one of the values is the key to the others. The EU solution is economy, the American principlist proposal autonomy, and the European principlist value dignity. I have expressed my doubts concerning these. Alternatively, we can admit the plurality and conflicts, and devise a prioritization plan, maybe along the lines of Finnis's practically reasonable decision-maker. Finnis's proposal will figure, indirectly, in my conclusions.

Other alliances between theories of justice produce a possibly eugenic liberal or social democracy and a feminist take on care and human rights. Apart from these, compromise views like justice as fairness by John Rawls have a natural space near the center of my map in Figures 1–4. None of these renounces capitalism or perpetual material growth, but Kittay's notion of dependency workers and Jaggar's concept of the normative human as female are clearly worth exploring further.

With this summary, I have exhausted the "is" and "should" dimensions of my two theses. The role of justice in bioethics does not seem to be to challenge continuous material growth, and I take this to confirm my first thesis, with the proviso that not all aspects of care ethics and utilitarianism have entered the story yet. The role of justice in bioethics should be to challenge continuous material growth, if we believe that ecologico-social equality or the conservation of decently livable human, nonhuman, and environmental circumstances is a priority of our time, as international declarations seem to testify. The remaining aspect, then, is the "can." Is there a combination of theories of justice that could deliver, even in theory? Insisting that we should do something that we cannot do would go against the traditional logic that "ought" implies "can."

9.2 An Outside-the-Box Alliance for Socio-Ecological Equality

The remaining alliance between theories of justice as interpretations of equality is between care ethics and utilitarianism, supported by luck egalitarian or socialist thinking. This is an unlikely union, but it combines the aspects that have been ignored by the views promoting or condoning only economic sustainability. It may offer a transition to the – so far evasive – ecologico-social equality that we seem to need.

In conceptualizing the alliance, we should avoid interpreting the theories of justice in the way they are interpreted by principlists, American or European. Conservative forms of feminism that support traditional gender roles should be excluded due to their potentially oppressive nature. More critical readings of care and relations are needed to replace them. The ideal of maximizing well-being should also be averted because there is a strong tendency to conflate it with economic indicators such as the gross national product. Minimizing suffering could be a viable alternative. And shared responsibility is probably a sufficient starting point for considering the libertarian-socialist juxtaposition.

Figure 5 presents the alliances for ecologico-social equality and economic sustainability. The triangle in the lower center marks the area that I am interested in.

In the economic-sustainability (upper) half of the map, a search for innovations, a feeling of excitement, and a pursuit of growth, with libertarian and capability ethics, suggest technology and business solutions in biomedicine, genetics, systems biology, nanotechnology, neuro enhancements, synthetic biology, and others. Old practices, precaution, and a quest for continuity, with libertarian and communitarian ethics, support traditional social and healthcare arrangements, which may be susceptible to sexism, paternalism, and discrimination. Compensation from the technology and business side may be needed to prevent political unrest in the old-fashioned circles. When, for instance, pharmaceutical trials in the Global South include benefit-sharing programs, one of their functions can be to recompense the violation of community customs.

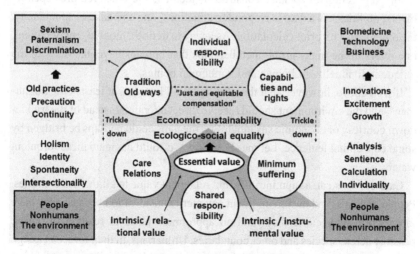

Figure 5 Economic sustainability and ecologico-social equality

In the (lower) ecologico-social equality half, doctrines of justice share a concern for all people, at least some nonhuman animals, and the natural environment. Theoretical disagreement has in the past prevented collaboration, however, and the care ethics and utilitarianism relationship is often icy. The dispute between Eva Feder Kittay and Jeff McMahan on the moral status of severely cognitively disabled human beings illustrates the matter. Kittay argues that any child born of a human mother is a proper object of our respect and protection;[211] McMahan holds that such respect and protection could be granted to organisms of any species that possess certain psychological capacities.[212] This is a slightly perplexing confrontation. McMahan seems to fear that nonhuman animals will be left without protections on Kittay's criterion. Kittay seems to worry that clever animals will be prioritized over severely cognitively disabled human beings, leaving the latter without care. McMahan's concern is valid only if Kittay had no regard for nonhumans; and Kittay's only if McMahan had no regard for severely cognitively disabled humans. Neither appears to be the case, and a practical agreement could, I believe, easily be forged between these views. We could respect and protect both mother-born human children, whatever their condition, and nonhuman animals who have the required mental capacities.[213] If microlevel questions of justice arise about the allocation of scarce resources among the groups, I suggest that they should be answered by other principles and considerations, anyway.[214]

That said, the theoretical differences between care ethics and utilitarianism are deep. As a way to acquire knowledge about things, one appeals to holistic insight, the other to linguistic analysis. As a way to single out entities with moral worth, one relies on socially constructed identity, the other requires specific mental abilities. As a way to respond to situations, one emphasizes spontaneity, the other banks on prior calculation. As a way to define a moral agent or patient, one refers to the many group memberships that humans have, the other to the unique individuality of human and nonhuman beings.

If we believe, however, that the equality of all humans, at least some nonhumans, and the environment should receive direct attention instead of the trickle-down courtesy of economic sustainability, the gaps could perhaps be bridged by some conceptual lenience. Let me show how we could navigate these turbulent waters.

Care ethicists can assign intrinsic and relational value to all the listed entities. People, animals, and the environment can merit consideration because they have inner worth or because they hold an appropriate place in relation to others, possibly across species and other boundaries. Utilitarians, in their turn, can assign intrinsic value at least to persons (entities aware of their own existence over time) and sentient beings (entities capable of feeling pain and pleasure). They could also recognize the innumerable interconnections between people, animals, and the environment, and assign nonpersons and non-sentient beings instrumental value even in cases where the connections are not immediately detectable.

For an agreement to emerge, all that would be needed is for philosophers in the two schools to agree on a conceptual moratorium. Utilitarians would have to turn a blind eye to the holistic and identity bases of the care and relations axiology. Care ethicists would have to ignore the linguistic and psychological emphasis of the utilitarian justification. The conceptual caveats duly noted and strategically forgotten, both could assign all life in its many forms essential value and build ecologico-social equality on this.

Lest I be accused of overlooking Kantian ethics, let me note that the word "bioethics" – or its German form "Bio-Ethik" – was first used by Fritz Jahr in 1926, long before the advent of the discipline as I have traced its origins here.[215] Jahr argued that a genuine life morality would extend Kant's categorical imperative to all animals and plants and replace the respect for persons with respect for every living being.[216] As for the history of the other approaches, virtue, or care, ethics has also operated on a more than anthropocentric theory of value at least since Albert Schweitzer's 1930 views on reverence for life, founded on a will to live as the natural goal of all organisms.[217] Utilitarians can claim an even longer ancestry in this, albeit limited to sentience, with Jeremy Bentham's famous dictum, "the question is not, Can they reason? nor, Can they talk? but, Can they suffer?" by which he included nonhuman animals in the realm of moral considerations.[218]

Two differences remain between care ethics and utilitarianism: spontaneity vs. calculation and intersectionality vs. individuality. On the former, perhaps reasonable people could agree that both are needed. We are here and now, and also later, so why not keep an eye out for both one and the other? On the latter, I would suggest that care ethicists widen the scope of intersectionality and utilitarians allow varied content in individuality. I am not just a *homo economicus*, an economically rational agent in pursuit of my own material self-interest, as some preference utilitarians would have it.[219] I am not just a woman or man, dependency worker or non-dependency worker, either. I belong to a plethora of visible and invisible groups defined by age, sexual orientation, culture, social background, and numerous other factors. If all my intersectionalities are counted, there are not many people who belong to my specific group. Maybe this array of relations and memberships is what could be called my individuality or uniqueness? If care ethicists and utilitarians could agree on something like this, it would strengthen the strategic alliance further.

9.3 The Methods of Resistance and Emancipation

It should be clear by now that the kind of justice I am looking for is institutional justice that operates primarily on the levels of legislation, policy-making, and social and global agreements and practices. For assessments of equity and fairness in specific research and bedside situations, there are the principles of beneficence, nonmaleficence, autonomy, dignity, integrity, and vulnerability, and their adjustments to real life with all its details.

My second thesis in this treatise states that the role of justice in bioethics should be to reclaim moral and political concepts for resistance and emancipation. In the section above, I tried to carve out a theoretical niche for such an endeavor. My final task is to outline the conceptual background against which the inevitability of continuous material growth could be challenged.

I do not want to proceed too formally, but I believe that the thinking here could benefit from a two-tier approach. The model that I have in mind is Henry Sidgwick's tactic in his 1874 classic *The Methods of Ethics*.[220] He first identified three fundamental ethical intuitions: justice (judgments must be made impartially), prudence (the future is as important as the present), and the universality of goodness (everybody's interests ought to count equally). Sidgwick believed that the right "method of ethics" should conform to all three, and after investigating alternatives he concluded that two moral doctrines, universalistic hedonism and rational egoism, pass the test.

Sidgwick's fundamental intuitions are consequentialist credos, and I am not suggesting that they could be used as such in our context. By "we" and "our," by the way, I refer to those who think that economic sustainability (as defined) should be complemented by ecologico-social equality (as sketched); who find my map of doctrines of justice credible; and who share my belief that care and relations ethics, a minimum-suffering version of utilitarianism, and shared social responsibility should enter the mix in constructing a theory for further work on justice in bioethics and in other fields.

The main "intuitions" that we need to include, it seems to me, are care and compassion from the care ethics camp, consequences and copathy from the utilitarian side, and some kind of camaraderie from the shared responsibility direction.

Care could best be conceptualized in terms of Kittay's dependency and dependency workers. Some need special care, some must provide it, and focusing on these groups is a good start for any future model for reaching ecologico-social equality. Extending the care to nonhuman animals and the environment would be desirable, either directly or at least indirectly, considering the consequences on them.

Compassion is an appropriate attitude toward dependency workers and the particularly dependent alike, but it has to be understood in terms of equality. A historical example to the contrary is the charitable attending to the sick and poor in medieval times, with the ethos that their suffering was their main claim to dignity and salvation. Sympathetic concern for the misfortunes of others, combined with an understanding of one's own dependency and vulnerability, is, I think, better for resistance and emancipation.

Consequences have to be understood more extensively than American principlism, in its fear of an excessively demanding ethic, would allow. Following the Belmont Report, the four-principles model warns against experiments that cause nonhuman animals unnecessary pain. In ecologico-social equality, the rule has to be applied further, in theory to all pain and anxiety that our acts and omissions can be expected to cause.

Copathy is an attitude that supports the wide consideration of consequences in terms of minimizing suffering. It is "a calm sensation or realization that we are one with all other sentient beings, and that we should not by our actions or choices make their lot worse."[221] This emotion is fully compatible with caring compassion and reminds us by its neutrality that stronger feelings like guilt, shame, pity, love, and hatred do not, and maybe should not, necessarily have to enter our decisions. This is a point at which we need to tread with caution, though. It is a distinctly liberal and utilitarian ideal to have neutrally impartial decision-makers.

I would like to use here the solution already used in the matter of intersectionality and individuality. Copathic decision-makers can have the calm sensation of unity with other beings, but they should also have an understanding and recognition of more intense feelings and attitudes. As Jaggar suggests,[222] we should not accept white, middle-aged, able-bodied, heterosexual, affluent (the list can go on) maleness as the seat of objective rationality and normative humanity, either in decision-makers or those affected by the decisions. Something like Finnis's practical reasonableness[223] would be good, with proper precautions in real-life applications.

Camaraderie would ideally be a joint agency by carers, reducers of suffering, dependents, and sufferers, all of which we may be at some point in our lives. It would be solidarity against indifference, disregard, non-recognition, discrimination, and oppression,[224] whether caused by deliberate, intentional actions or by the silent and unquestioned acceptance of an economic and political system that keeps us subordinated, inflicts harm on nonhuman animals, and causes environmental degradation.

On these five intuitions, I would build a new institution-level account of justice in bioethics. An important additional requirement is that the model should not become a "utilitarianism of care" – this would go too strongly against the thinking of the less calculative partners of the alliance. A "caring conse-quentialism" could be closer. In my research circle, Maarit Laihonen is devel-oping this possibility in her account of "prefigurative utilitarianism."[225] Tentatively, this creed does not condone the use of means if they do not align with the ends yet expects the good of all to be the primary aim of our actions. Will this, or similar attempts,[226] succeed? Time will tell. In the meantime, I conclude that I have supported, as far as I think that they can be supported, my two theses, and my work here is done.

Notes

1. Nutton 2013.
2. Miller 1997.
3. Pormann & Savage-Smith 2007.
4. Porter 1997.
5. Schendel 1968, 99.
6. Numbers 2009, 45.
7. Kirby 1983; Häyry & Takala 2001b.
8. Mackowiak & Sehdev 2002.
9. Davis & Warner 1918, 2–5.
10. Percival 1803.
11. Patuzzo, Goracci, & Ciliberti 2018.
12. Patuzzo, Goracci, & Ciliberti 2018.
13. Baker & Emanuel 2000.
14. Schroeder-Lein 2008.
15. Magnello 2012.
16. Madigan, Martinko, & Brock 2006.
17. Buchanan, Brock, Daniels, & Wikler 2000.
18. Beisel & Kay 2004; Baker 2013.
19. Mohr 1978.
20. Hayward 2011.
21. Häyry 2021a.
22. Mettraux 2008.
23. The Nuremberg Code (1947) 1996.
24. Faden 1996.
25. Notably, Andrew Ivy – https://en.wikipedia.org/wiki/Andrew_Conway_Ivy.
26. Brandt 1978.
27. World Medical Association 1947.
28. World Medical Association 2018.
29. Jonsen 1998.
30. Jonsen 1998, viii–ix.
31. Childress 1971.
32. Singer 1973.
33. Jonsen 1998, x–ix.
34. Häyry & Häyry 1998.
35. Jonsen 1998, 11.
36. Häyry 1990; Häyry 1994a.
37. Mazur 2011.
38. Pellegrino 1979.
39. Pellegrino & Thomasma 1993.
40. The Belmont Report 1979.
41. Beauchamp & Childress 2001. I will use this, fifth, edition, for comparative purposes, until Section 5.2.2, where I will switch to the latest edition.

42. Macklin 1999.
43. Thomson 1971.
44. Warren 1973.
45. Mothersill 1971.
46. Foot 1977.
47. Singer 1979.
48. Singer & Wells 1984.
49. Kuhse & Singer 1985.
50. Singer & Cavalieri 1993.
51. Glover 1977.
52. Harris 1985.
53. Hursthouse 1987.
54. O'Neill 1986.
55. Maclean 1993.
56. Kittay 1999.
57. Oderberg 2000.
58. Jackson 2006.
59. Smart & Williams 1973.
60. Anscombe 1957.
61. Gillon 1985.
62. Childress 1982.
63. Kleinig 1983.
64. Häyry, H. 1991.
65. Häyry & Häyry 1990.
66. Häyry & Häyry 1989.
67. Häyry, Takala, & Herissone-Kelly 2007.
68. Takala 2000; Häyry & Takala 2001a; Häyry 2001; Häyry 2007a: Häyry 2018a.
69. Lederberg 1966.
70. Ramsey 1970.
71. Fletcher 1974.
72. Agar 2004.
73. Rhodes 1998.
74. Takala & Häyry 2000.
75. Chadwick 1982.
76. Häyry 2002; Häyry 2007b.
77. Häyry 2003; Häyry & Takala 2007.
78. Beauchamp & Childress 2001, 227.
79. Beauchamp & Childress 2001, 228.
80. Beauchamp & Childress 2001, 230.
81. Beauchamp & Childress 2001, 231.
82. Beauchamp & Childress 2001, 231–2.
83. Beauchamp & Childress 2001, 232–3.
84. Beauchamp & Childress 2001, 233–5.
85. Beauchamp & Childress 2001, 234; Daniels 1985, 34–58.
86. Beauchamp & Childress 2001, 235–7.

87. Buchanan, Brock, Daniels, and Wikler 2000.
88. Nelson & Nelson 2001.
89. Häyry 2003; Häyry & Takala 2007.
90. Häyry & Takala 2022.
91. MacIntyre 1981.
92. Holm 1995.
93. Gillon 1985.
94. Singer 2011, viii–ix.
95. Rendtorff & Kemp 2000, 393–9.
96. Rendtorff & Kemp 2000, 358–9.
97. Rendtorff & Kemp 2000, 359.
98. Rendtorff & Kemp 2000, 359.
99. Rendtorff & Kemp 2000, 359.
100. Rendtorff & Kemp 2000, 360.
101. Rendtorff & Kemp 2000, 360.
102. Rendtorff & Kemp 2000, 131.
103. Harris 1987; Häyry, M. 1991.
104. Rendtorff & Kemp 2000, 361.
105. Häyry 2018b.
106. Rendtorff & Kemp 2000, 132.
107. Dworkin 1981a; Dworkin 1981b; Cohen 1989.
108. Anderson 1999.
109. Ahola-Launonen 2018.
110. Rendtorff & Kemp 2000, 359.
111. Häyry 2005.
112. Beauchamp & Childress 2001, 233.
113. Ritner 1967.
114. Häyry 2012.
115. Beauchamp & Childress 2001, 233.
116. Häyry 2018b.
117. Beauchamp & Childress 2001, 369–76.
118. Gilligan 1982.
119. Beauchamp & Childress 2001, 371.
120. Baier 1985.
121. Sherwin 1992.
122. Beauchamp & Childress 2001, 375–6.
123. Beauchamp & Childress 2019, 277–9.
124. Beauchamp & Childress 2019, 278; Nussbaum 2006, 76–8.
125. Beauchamp & Childress 2019, 279.
126. Häyry 2011.
127. Rhodes, Battin, & Silvers 2002. Also, e.g., Häyry, Takala, & Herissone-Kelly 2005.
128. Häyry 2007c, 24–6.
129. Häyry, Chadwick, Árnason, & Árnason 2007.
130. Häyry & Takala 2005.
131. Takala 2001.

132. Häyry & Takala 2022.
133. Green, Donovan, & Jauss 2008.
134. Häyry, Takala, & Herissone-Kelly 2005.
135. Widdows, Dickenson, & Hellsten 2003; Hellsten 2008; Widdows 2011.
136. Luna 2006.
137. Qiu 2004.
138. Tangwa 2019.
139. Häyry, Takala, & Herissone-Kelly 2007.
140. Häyry & Vehmas 2015.
141. Häyry & Vehmas 2015.
142. Takala 2001.
143. Häyry & Vehmas 2015, 94.
144. Gross 2021.
145. Gross 2021.
146. Gross 2021.
147. Nussbaum 1995.
148. Hamington & Sander-Staudt 2011.
149. Firestone 1970.
150. Mahowald 1988.
151. Smith 1904.
152. Marx & Engels 2004.
153. Johnson No date.
154. Häyry & Laihonen, forthcoming.
155. United Nations 2015; Kopnina 2016.
156. Lang & Pye 2000.
157. Lang and Pye 2000.
158. Osborn 1948.
159. Vogt 1948.
160. Ehrlich & Ehrlich 1968.
161. Desrochers & Hoffbauer 2009.
162. Buchanan, Brock, Daniels, & Wikler 2000; Häyry 2008; Häyry 2010.
163. Klausen & Bashford 2010.
164. Ryan 1911.
165. Gardner 2010.
166. European Commission 2018, 4.
167. Desrochers & Hoffbauer 2009.
168. Meadows, Meadows, Randers, & Behrens 1972; Mesarovic & Pestel 1974.
169. Vermeulen & De Jongh 1976; Mihram 1977.
170. Schiermeier 2018.
171. Randers et al. 2018.
172. Randers et al. 2018.
173. Najam 2005.
174. IUCN 1980.
175. IUCN 1980.
176. United Nations 1987, 37.

177. Anker 2018.
178. United Nations 2015, 14; Häyry & Laihonen forthcoming.
179. Whelan 2010.
180. Häyry et al. 2021.
181. European Commission 2018, 4; Häyry & Laihonen forthcoming.
182. Häyry et al. 2021; Häyry & Laihonen forthcoming.
183. Stevis-Gridneff 2019.
184. Finnis 2011.
185. Crowe 2014.
186. Mendelsohn 1996.
187. Finnis 2011, 15.
188. Buchanan, Brock, Daniels, and Wikler 2000; Savulescu 2001; Agar 2004; McMahan 2005; Glover 2006; Green 2007; Harris 2007.
189. Kass 2002; Habermas 2003; Sandel 2007.
190. Chadwick 1989; Häyry 1994b.
191. Häyry 2010.
192. Häyry 2008.
193. Häyry 2008, 20.
194. Häyry 2008, 20.
195. Häyry 2008, 17.
196. Häyry 2008, 19–20.
197. Beecher & Stowe 1971.
198. Buhle & Buhle 1978.
199. Häyry 2019.
200. Mill 1996.
201. Presley & Sartwell 2005; Riggenbach 2014.
202. Tong & Williams 2002.
203. Kittay 1999; Tong & Williams 2002.
204. Kittay & Feder 2002.
205. Jaggar 2002.
206. Jaggar 2002, 366; Nussbaum 1995, 72–5.
207. Jaggar 2002, 367.
208. Jaggar 2002, 368.
209. Jaggar 2002, 372.
210. Jaggar 2002, 368.
211. Kittay 1999.
212. McMahan 2005.
213. Häyry 2016.
214. Häyry 1990; Häyry 1994a.
215. Jahr 2017.
216. Jahr 2011.
217. Barsam 2008.
218. Bentham 1982, 283 note b.
219. Harsanyi 1982.
220. Sidgwick 1981.
221. Häyry 2022a.

222. Jaggar 2002, 368.
223. Finnis 2011, 15.
224. Häyry 2022b.
225. Laihonen 2020.
226. Häyry 1994a; Häyry 2021b.

References

Agar, Nicholas. *Liberal Eugenics: In Defence of Human Enhancement*. Oxford: Blackwell Publishing, 2004.

Ahola-Launonen, Johanna. *Hijacking Responsibility: Philosophical Studies on Health Distribution*. Helsinki: University of Helsinki, 2018.

Anderson, Elizabeth S. What Is the Point of Equality? *Ethics* 109 (1999): 287–337.

Anker, Peder. A Pioneer Country? A History of Norwegian Climate Politics. *Climatic Change* 151 (2018): 29–41. https://doi.org/10.1007/s10584-016-1653-x.

Anscombe, G. E. M. Does Oxford Moral Philosophy Corrupt the Youth? *The Listener* February 14, 1957: 266–71.

Baier, Annette C. What Do Women Want in a Moral Theory? *Nous* 19 (1985): 53–63.

Baker, Robert. *Before Bioethics: A History of American Medical Ethics from the Colonial Period to the Bioethics Revolution*. New York: Oxford University Press, 2013.

Baker, Robert, and Emanuel, Linda. The Efficacy of Professional Ethics: The AMA Code of Ethics in Historical and Current Perspective. *The Hastings Center Report* 30 (2000): 13–17. https://doi.org/10.2307/3527657.

Barsam, Ara Paul. *Reverence for Life: Albert Schweitzer's Great Contribution to Ethical Thought*. New York: Oxford University Press, 2008.

Beauchamp, Tom L., and Childress, James F. *Principles of Biomedical Ethics*. 5th ed. Oxford: Oxford University Press, 2001.

Beauchamp, Tom L., and Childress, James F. *Principles of Biomedical Ethics*. 8th ed. Oxford: Oxford University Press, 2019.

Beecher, Catharine, and Stowe, Harriet. *American Woman's Home: Or, Principles of Domestic Science: Being a Guide to the Formation and Maintenance of Economical, Healthful, Beautiful, and Christian Homes* (original 1869). New York: Aeno Press and *The New York Times*, 1971.

Beisel, Nicola, and Kay, Tamara. Abortion, Race, and Gender in Nineteenth-Century America. *American Sociological Review* 69 (2004): 498–518. https://doi.org/10.1177/000312240406900402.

The Belmont Report: Ethical Principles and Guidelines for the Protection of Human Subjects of Research. Washington, D.C.: National Commission for the Protection of Human Subjects of Biomedical and Behavioral Research, 1979.

Bentham, Jeremy. *An Introduction to the Principles of Morals and Legislation* (original 1789). Burns, J. H., and Hart, H. L. A., eds. London: Methuen, 1982.

Brandt, Allan M. Racism and Research: The Case of the Tuskegee Syphilis Study. *The Hastings Center Report* 8 (1978): 21–9. https://doi.org/10.2307/3561468.

Buchanan, Allen, Brock, Dan W., Daniels, Norman, and Wikler, Daniel. *From Chance to Choice: Genetics and Justice*. Cambridge: Cambridge University Press, 2000.

Buhle, Mari Jo, and Buhle, Paul, eds. *The Concise History of Woman Suffrage: Selections from History of Woman Suffrage*. Urbana: University of Illinois Press, 1978.

Chadwick, Ruth. Cloning. *Philosophy* 57 (1982): 201–9.

Chadwick, Ruth F. Playing God. *Cogito* 3 (1989): 186–93. https://doi.org/10.5840/cogito19893347.

Childress, James F. *Civil Disobedience and Moral Obligation: A Study in Christian Social Ethics*. New Haven, CT: Yale University Press, 1971.

Childress, James F. *Who Should Decide? Paternalism in Health Care*. Oxford: Oxford University Press, 1982.

Cohen, Gerald A. On the Currency of Egalitarian Justice. *Ethics* 99 (1989): 906–44.

Crowe, Jonathan. Reason, Morality, and Law: The Philosophy of John Finnis. *Notre Dame Philosophical Reviews* March 14, 2014. https://ndpr.nd.edu/news/46786-reason-morality-and-law-the-philosophy-of-john-finnis/.

Daniels, Norman. *Just Health Care*. New York: Cambridge University Press, 1985.

Davis, Michael Marks, and Warner, Andrew Robert. *Dispensaries, Their Management and Development: A Book for Administrators, Public Health Workers, and All Interested in Better Medical Service for the People*. New York: MacMillan, 1918.

Desrochers, Pierre, and Christine Hoffbauer. The Post War Intellectual Roots of the Population Bomb: Fairfield Osborn's "Our Plundered Planet" and William Vogt's "Road to Survival" in Retrospect. *The Electronic Journal of Sustainable Development* 1 (2009). www.researchgate.net/publication/253375313_The_Post_War_Intellectual_Roots_of_the_Population_Bomb_Fairfield_Osborn%27s_%27Our_Plundered_Planet%27_and_William_Vogt%27s_%27Road_to_Survival%27_in_Retrospect.

Dworkin, Ronald. What Is Equality? Part 1: Equality of Welfare. *Philosophy & Public Affairs* 10 (1981a): 185–246.

Dworkin, Ronald. What Is Equality? Part 2: Equality of Resources. *Philosophy & Public Affairs* 10 (1981b): 283–345.

Ehrlich, Paul [and Ehrlich, Anne, uncredited]. *The Population Bomb.* New York: Buccaneer Books, 1968.

European Commission. *A Sustainable Bioeconomy for Europe: Strengthening the Connection between Economy, Society and the Environment: Updated Bioeconomy Strategy.* 2018. https://op.europa.eu/en/publication-detail/-/publication/edace3e3-e189-11e8-b690-01aa75ed71a1/language-en/format-PDF/source-214335575.

Faden, Ruth. The Advisory Committee on Human Radiation Experiments: Reflections on a Presidential Commission. *Hastings Center Report* 26 (1996): 5–10. https://doi.org/10.2307/3528463.

Finnis, John. *Natural Law and Natural Rights* (original 1980). 2nd ed. Oxford: Oxford University Press, 2011.

Firestone, Shulamith. *The Dialectic of Sex: The Case for a Feminist Revolution.* New York: William Morrow and Company, 1970.

Fletcher, Joseph. *The Ethics of Genetic Control: Ending Reproductive Roulette.* Garden City, NY: Anchor Press, 1974.

Foot, Philippa. Euthanasia. *Philosophy & Public Affairs* 6 (1977): 85–112.

Gardner, Dan. *Future Babble: Why Expert Predictions Fail – and Why We Believe Them Anyway.* Toronto: McClelland and Stewart, 2010.

Gilligan, Carol. *In a Different Voice: Psychological Theory and Women's Development.* Cambridge, MA: Harvard University Press, 1982.

Gillon, Raanan. *Philosophical Medical Ethics.* Chichester: John Wiley & Sons, 1985.

Glover, Jonathan. *Causing Death and Saving Lives.* Harmondsworth: Penguin Books, 1977.

Glover, Jonathan. *Choosing Children: Genes, Disability and Design.* Oxford: Oxford University Press, 2006.

Green, Ronald. *Babies by Design: The Ethics of Genetic Choice.* New Haven, CT: Yale University Press, 2007.

Green, Ronald, Donovan, Aine, and Jauss, Steven, eds. *Global Bioethics: Issues of Conscience for the Twenty-First Century.* Oxford: Clarendon Press, 2008.

Gross, Daniel A. Peter Singer Is Committed to Controversial Ideas. *The New Yorker* April 25, 2021.

Habermas, Jürgen. *The Future of Human Nature.* Translated by William Rehg, Max Pensky, and Hella Beister. Cambridge: Polity Press, 2003.

Hamington, Maurice, and Sander-Staudt, Maureen, eds. *Applying Care Ethics to Business.* Cham: Springer, 2011.

Harris, John. *The Value of Life: An Introduction to Medical Ethics.* London: Routledge & Kegan Paul, 1985.

Harris, John. QALYfying the Value of Life. *Journal of Medical Ethics* 13 (1987): 117–23.

Harris, John. *Enhancing Evolution: The Ethical Case for Making Better People.* Princeton, NJ: Princeton University Press, 2007.

Harsanyi, John. Morality and the Theory of Rational Behaviour. In Amartya Sen and Bernard Williams, eds. *Utilitarianism and Beyond.* Cambridge: Cambridge University Press, 1982: 39–62.

Häyry, Heta. *The Limits of Medical Paternalism.* London: Routledge, 1991.

Häyry, Heta, and Häyry, Matti. Applied Philosophy at the Turn of the Millennium. In Oliver Leaman, ed. *The Future of Philosophy: Towards the 21st Century.* London: Routledge, 1998: 90–104.

Häyry, Matti. *Critical Studies in Philosophical Medical Ethics.* Helsinki: University of Helsinki, 1990.

Häyry, Matti. Measuring the Quality of Life: Why, How and What? *Theoretical Medicine* 12 (1991): 97–116.

Häyry, Matti. *Liberal Utilitarianism and Applied Ethics.* London: Routledge, 1994a.

Häyry, Matti. Categorical Objections to Genetic Engineering – A Critique. In Anthony Dyson and John Harris, eds. *Ethics and Biotechnology.* London: Routledge, 1994b: 202–15.

Häyry, Matti. But What If We Feel That Cloning Is Wrong? *Cambridge Quarterly of Healthcare Ethics* 10 (2001): 205–8.

Häyry, Matti. Utilitarian Approaches to Justice in Health Care. In Rosamond Rhodes, Margaret P. Battin, and Anita Silvers, eds. *Medicine and Social Justice: Essays on the Distribution of Health Care.* New York: Oxford University Press, 2002: 53–64.

Häyry, Matti. European Values in Bioethics: Why, What, and How to Be Used? *Theoretical Medicine and Bioethics* 24 (2003): 199–214.

Häyry, Matti. The Tension between Self-Governance and Absolute Inner Worth in Kant's Moral Philosophy. *Journal of Medical Ethics* 31 (2005): 645–7.

Häyry, Matti. *Cloning, Selection, and Values: Essays on Bioethical Intuitions.* Helsinki: Acta Philosophica Fennica Vol. 81, 2007a.

Häyry, Matti. Utilitarianism and Bioethics. In Richard Ashcroft, Angus Dawson, Heather Draper, and John McMillan, eds. *Principles of Health Care Ethics.* 2nd ed. Chichester: John Wiley & Sons, 2007b: 57–64.

Häyry, Matti. Some Current Issues in the Ethics of Biomedical Research and Their Background in the Protection of the Dignity and Autonomy of the Vulnerable. In Matti Häyry, Tuija Takala, and Peter Herissone-Kelly, eds. *Ethics in Biomedical Research: International Perspectives.* Amsterdam: Brill, 2007c: 21–32.

Häyry, Matti. The Historical Idea of a Better Race. *Studies in Ethics, Law, and Technology* 2 (2008), article 11. www.researchgate.net/publication/40823116_ The_Historical_Idea_of_a_Better_Race.

Häyry, Matti. *Rationality and the Genetic Challenge: Making People Better?* Cambridge: Cambridge University Press, 2010.

Häyry, Matti. Considerable Life Extension and Three Views on the Meaning of Life. *Cambridge Quarterly of Healthcare Ethics* 20 (2011): 21–9.

Häyry, Matti. Protecting Humanity: Habermas and His Critics on the Ethics of Emerging Technologies. *Cambridge Quarterly of Healthcare Ethics* 21 (2012): 211–22.

Häyry, Matti. Discoursive Humanity as a Transcendental Basis for Cognitive-(Dis) Ability Ethics and Policies. *Cambridge Quarterly of Healthcare Ethics* 25 (2016): 262–71.

Häyry, Matti. Ethics and Cloning. *British Medical Bulletin* 128 (2018a): 15–21. https://doi.org/10.1093/bmb/ldy031.

Häyry, Matti. Doctrines and Dimensions of Justice: Their Historical Backgrounds and Ideological Underpinnings. *Cambridge Quarterly of Healthcare Ethics* 27 (2018b): 188–216.

Häyry, Matti. Justice and the Possibility of Good Moralism. *Cambridge Quarterly of Healthcare Ethics* 28 (2019): 236–263.

Häyry, Matti. The COVID-19 Pandemic: A Month of Bioethics in Finland. *Cambridge Quarterly of Healthcare Ethics* 30 (2021a): 114–122. https://doi .org/10.1017/S0963180120000432.

Häyry, Matti. Just Better Utilitarianism. *Cambridge Quarterly of Healthcare Ethics* 30 (2021b): 343–67. Published online December 7, 2020. https://doi .org/10.1017/S0963180120000882.

Häyry, Matti. COVID-19 and Beyond: The Need for Copathy and Impartial Advisers. *Cambridge Quarterly of Healthcare Ethics* 31 (2022a), forthcoming. Published online February 22, 2021. https://doi.org/10.1017/S096318012 1000013.

Häyry, Matti. COVID-19: Another Look at Solidarity. *Cambridge Quarterly of Healthcare Ethics* 31 (2022b), forthcoming. Published online December 21, 2020. https://doi.org/10.1017/S0963180120001115.

Häyry, Matti, Ahola-Launonen, Johanna, Kurki, Sofi, Laihonen, Maarit, Porttikivi, Merja, Balcom Raleigh, Nicolas, Taylor, Amos, Saarenmaa, Liisa, Takala, Tuija, and Wilenius, Markku. Planeetan elinkelpoisuus, biotalous ja oikeudenmukaisuus – hyvän ja pahan tiedon rajat [Planetary Livability, Bioeconomy, and Justice – The Limits of Good and Bad Knowledge, in Finnish]. In Ilari Hetemäki, Anna-Kaisa Kuusisto, Marja Lähteenmäki, and

Esa Väliverronen, eds. *Hyvä ja paha tieto* [*Good and Bad Knowledge*]. Helsinki: Gaudeamus, 2021: 248–61.

Häyry, Matti, Chadwick, Ruth, Árnason, Vilhjálmur, and Árnason, Gardar, eds. *The Ethics and Governance of Human Genetic Databases: European Perspectives*. Cambridge: Cambridge University Press, 2007.

Häyry, Matti, and Häyry, Heta. AIDS, Society, and Morality – A Philosophical Survey. *Philosophia* 19 (1989): 331–61. https://doi.org/10.1007/BF02380 272.

Häyry, Matti, and Häyry, Heta. Health Care as a Right, Fairness and Medical Resources. *Bioethics* 4 (1990): 1–21.

Häyry, Matti, and Laihonen, Maarit. Situating a Sustainable Bioeconomy Strategy on a Map of Justice: A Solution and Its Problems, forthcoming.

Häyry, Matti, and Takala, Tuija. Cloning, Naturalness and Personhood. In David C. Thomasma, David N. Weisstub, and Christian Hervé, eds. *Personhood and Health Care*. Dordrecht: Kluwer Academic Publishers, 2001a: 281–98.

Häyry, Matti, and Takala, Tuija. Genetic Information, Rights, and Autonomy. *Theoretical Medicine and Bioethics* 22 (2001b): 403–14.

Häyry, Matti, and Takala, Tuija. Human Dignity, Bioethics, and Human Rights. *Developing World Bioethics* 5 (2005): 225–33.

Häyry, Matti, and Takala, Tuija. American Principles, European Values, and the Mezzanine Rules of Ethical Genetic Data Banking. In Matti Häyry, Ruth Chadwick, Vilhjálmur Árnason, and Gardar Árnason, eds. *The Ethics and Governance of Human Genetic Databases: European Perspectives*. Cambridge: Cambridge University Press, 2007: 14–36.

Häyry, Matti, and Takala, Tuija, eds. Common Morality. *Cambridge Quarterly of Healthcare Ethics* 31 (2022): 161–219.

Häyry, Matti, Takala, Tuija, and Herissone-Kelly, Peter, eds. *Bioethics and Social Reality*. Amsterdam: Brill, 2005.

Häyry, Matti, Takala, Tuija, and Herissone-Kelly, Peter, eds. *Ethics in Biomedical Research: International Perspectives*. Amsterdam: Brill, 2007.

Häyry, Matti, and Vehmas, Simo. Disability as a Test of Justice in a Globalising World. *Journal of Global Ethics* 11 (2015): 90–8.

Hayward, Rhodri. Medicine and the Mind. In Mark Jackson, ed. *The Oxford Handbook of the History of Medicine*. Oxford: Oxford University Press, 2011: 524–42.

Hellsten, Sirkku K. Global Bioethics: Utopia or Reality? *Developing World Bioethics* 8 (2008): 70–81.

Holm, Søren. Not Just Autonomy – the Principles of American Biomedical Ethics. *Journal of Medical Ethics* 21 (1995): 332–8.

Hursthouse, Rosalind. *Beginning Lives*. Oxford: Basil Blackwell, 1987.

IUCN – International Union for Conservation of Nature and Natural Resources. *World Conservation Strategy: Living Resource Conservation for Sustainable Development*. 1980. https://portals.iucn.org/library/efiles/documents/wcs-004.pdf.

Jackson, Jennifer. *Ethics in Medicine: Virtue, Vice and Medicine*. Cambridge: Polity Press, 2006.

Jaggar, Alison M. Feminist Ethics. In Hugh LaFollette, ed. *The Blackwell Guide to Ethical Theory*. Oxford: Blackwell Publishing, 2002: 348–74.

Jahr, Fritz. Bio-Ethics: Reviewing the Ethical Relations of Humans towards Animals and Plants [original 1927]. In Amir Muzur and Hans-Martin Sass, eds. *Fritz Jahr and the Foundations of Global Bioethics: The Future of Integrative Bioethics*. Zürich: Lit Verlag, 2011: 1–4.

Jahr, Fritz. Life Sciences and the Teaching of Ethics: Old Knowledge in New Clothing [original 1926]. Translated by Irene M. Miller. In Amir Muzur and Hans-Martin Sass, eds. *1926-2016 Fritz Jahr's Bioethics: A Global Discourse*. Zürich: Lit, 2017: 127–9.

Johnson, Ben. The Great Horse Manure Crisis of 1894. *Historic UK*. No date. www.historic-uk.com/HistoryUK/HistoryofBritain/Great-Horse-Manure-Crisis-of-1894/.

Jonsen, Albert R. *The Birth of Bioethics*. Oxford: Oxford University Press, 1998.

Kass, Leon. *Life, Liberty, and the Defense of Dignity: The Challenge for Bioethics*. San Francisco, CA: Encounter Books, 2002.

Kirby, Michael D. Informed Consent: What Does It Mean? *Journal of Medical Ethics* 9 (1983): 69–75.

Kittay, Eva Feder. *Love's Labor: Essays on Women, Equality, and Dependency*. New York: Routledge, 1999.

Kittay, Eva Feder, and Feder, Ellen K., eds. *The Subject of Care: Feminist Perspectives on Dependency*. Lanham, MD: Rowman & Littlefield Publishers, 2002.

Klausen, Susanne, and Bashford, Alison. Fertility Control: Eugenics, Neo-Malthusianism, and Feminism. In Alison Bashford and Philippa Levine, eds. *The Oxford Handbook of the History of Eugenics*. Oxford: Oxford University Press, 2010: 98–115.

Kleinig, John. *Paternalism*. Manchester: Manchester University Press, 1983.

Kopnina, Helen. The Victims of Unsustainability: A Challenge to Sustainable Development Goals. *International Journal of Sustainable Development & World Ecology* 23 (2016): 113–21. www.tandfonline.com/doi/full/10.1080/13504509.2015.1111269.

Kuhse, Helga, and Singer, Peter. *Should the Baby Live? The Problem of Handicapped Infants*. Oxford: Oxford University Press, 1985.

Laihonen, Maarit. *Suoran toiminnan oikeutus* [*A Justification of Direct Action*, in Finnish]. Helsinki: University of Helsinki, Faculty of Social Sciences, 2020. http://urn.fi/URN:NBN:fi:hulib-202012285511.

Lang, Chris, and Pye, Oliver. Blinded by Science: The Invention of Scientific Forestry and Its Influence in the Mekong Region. *Watershed* 6 (2000): 25–34. https://chrislang.org/2000/11/01/blinded-by-science-the-invention-of-scientific-forestry-and-its-influence-in-the-mekong-region/.

Lederberg, Joshua. Experimental Genetics and Human Evolution. *The American Naturalist* 100 (1966): 519–31.

Luna, Florencia, ed. *Bioethics and Vulnerability: A Latin American View*. Amsterdam: Brill, 2006.

MacIntyre, Alasdair. *After Virtue: A Study in Moral Theory*. London: Duckworth, 1981.

Macklin, Ruth. *Against Relativism: Cultural Diversity and the Search for Ethical Universals in Medicine*. Oxford: Oxford University Press, 1999.

Mackowiak, Philip A., and Sehdev, Paul S. The Origin of Quarantine. *Clinical Infectious Diseases* 35 (2002): 1071–2. https://doi.org/10.1086/344062.

Maclean, Anne. *The Elimination of Morality: Reflections on Utilitarianism and Bioethics*. London: Routledge, 1993.

Madigan, Michael T., Martinko, John M., and Brock, Thomas D. *Brock Biology of Microorganisms*. Eleventh edition. Englewood Cliffs, N.J.: Prentice-Hall, 2006.

Magnello, M. Eileen. Victorian Statistical Graphics and the Iconography of Florence Nightingale's Polar Area Graph. *BSHM Bulletin: Journal of the British Society for the History of Mathematics* 27 (2012): 13–37. https://doi.org/10.1080/17498430.2012.618102.

Mahowald, Mary B. Marx, Moral Judgment, and Medical Ethics: Commentary on Buchanan. In Baruch B. Brody, ed. *Moral Theory and Moral Judgments in Medical Ethics*. Dordrecht: Springer, 1988: 119–131. https://doi.org/10.1007/978-94-009-2715-5_10.

Marx, Karl, and Engels, Friedrich. *Manifesto of the Communist Party* [original 1848]. In *Selected Works* Vol. 1. Translated by Samuel Moore and Friedrich Engels, corr. Andy Blunden. Moscow: Progress Publishers, 2004: 98–137.

Mazur, Grzegorz. The Major Current Interpretations of the Principle of Free and Informed Consent. In Grzegorz Mazur, ed. *Informed Consent, Proxy Consent, and Catholic Bioethics: For the Good of the Subject*. Cham: Springer, 2011: 49–80.

McMahan, Jeff. Preventing the Existence of People with Disabilities. In David Wasserman, Jerome Bickenbach, and Robert Wachbroit, eds. *Quality of Life and Human Difference: Genetic Testing, Health Care, and Disability.* New York: Cambridge University Press, 2005: 142–71.

Meadows, Donella H., Meadows, Dennis L., Randers, Jørgen, and Behrens, William W., III. *The Limits to Growth: A Report for the Club of Rome's Project on the Predicament of Mankind.* New York: Universe Books, 1972.

Mendelsohn, Daniel. Expert Witnesses and Ancient Mysteries in a Colorado Courtroom. *Lingua Franca* September/October 1996. http://linguafranca .mirror.theinfo.org/9609/stand.html.

Mesarovic, Mihajlo, and Pestel, Eduard. *Mankind at the Turning Point: The Second Report to the Club of Rome.* New York: E. P. Dutton & Co., 1974.

Mettraux, Guénaël, ed. *Perspectives on the Nuremberg Trial.* Oxford: Oxford University Press, 2008.

Mihram, G. Arthur. Mankind at the Turning Point – Mihajlo Mesarovic and Eduard Pestel. *IEEE Transactions on Systems, Man, and Cybernetics* 7 (1977): 73–4.

Mill, John Stuart. *On Liberty and The Subjection of Women* [originals 1859 and 1869]. Ware, Hertfordshire: Wordsworth, 1996.

Miller, Timothy S. *The Birth of the Hospital in the Byzantine Empire.* Second edition. Baltimore, MD: Johns Hopkins University Press, 1997.

Mohr, James C. *Abortion in America: The Origins and Evolution of National Policy, 1800–1900.* New York: Oxford University Press, 1978.

Mothersill, Mary. Death. In James Rachels, ed. *Moral Problems: A Collection of Philosophical Essays.* New York: Harper & Row, 1971: 372–83.

Najam, Adil. Developing Countries and Global Environmental Governance: From Contestation to Participation to Engagement. *International Environmental Agreements: Politics, Law and Economics* 5 (2005): 303–21. https://doi.org/10 .1007/s10784-005-3807-6.

Nelson, James Lindemann, and Nelson, Hilde Lindemann. From Chance to Choice: Genetics and Justice (Review). *American Journal of Bioethics* 1 (2001): 70–2.

Numbers, Ronald L., ed. *Galileo Goes to Jail and Other Myths About Science and Religion.* Harvard, MA: Harvard University Press, 2009.

The Nuremberg Code (1947). *British Medical Journal* 313 (1996): 1448.

Nussbaum, Martha. Human Capabilities, Female Human Beings. In Martha Nussbaum and Jonathan Glover, eds. *Women, Culture, and Development.* Oxford: Clarendon Press, 1995: 61–104.

Nussbaum, Martha C. *Frontiers of Justice: Disability, Nationality, Species Membership.* Cambridge, MA: The Belknap Press of Harvard University Press, 2006.

Nutton, Vivian. *Ancient Medicine*. Revised edition. London: Routledge, 2013.

Oderberg, David S. *Applied Ethics: A Non-Consequentialist Approach*. Oxford: Blackwell, 2000.

O'Neill, Onora. *Faces of Hunger: An Essay on Poverty, Justice, and Development*. London: Allen & Unwin, 1986.

Osborn, Fairfield. *Our Plundered Planet*. Boston, MA: Little, Brown and Company, 1948.

Patuzzo, Sara, Goracci, Giada, and Ciliberti, Rosagemma. Thomas Percival: Discussing the Foundation of Medical Ethics. *Acta Biomedica* 89 (2018): 343–8. doi: 10.23750/abm.v89i3.7050.

Pellegrino, Edmund D. *Humanism and the Physician*. Knoxville: The University of Tennessee Press, 1979.

Pellegrino, Edmund D., and Thomasma, David C. *The Virtues in Medical Practice*. Oxford: Oxford University Press, 1993.

Percival, Thomas. *Medical Ethics*. Manchester: S. Russell for J. Johnson and R. Bickerstaff, 1803. https://archive.org/details/b21935014/page/n9/mode/2up.

Pormann, Peter E., and Savage-Smith, Emilie. *Medieval Islamic Medicine*. Edinburgh: Edinburgh University Press, 2007.

Porter, Roy. *The Greatest Benefit to Mankind: A Medical History of Humanity from Antiquity to the Present*. London: HarperCollins, 1997.

Presley, Sharon, and Sartwell, Crispin, ed. *Exquisite Rebel: The Essays of Voltairine de Cleyre – Anarchist, Feminist, Genius*. Albany, NY: SUNY Press, 2005.

Qiu, Ren-Zong, ed. *Bioethics: Asian Perspectives – A Quest for Moral Diversity*. Cham: Springer, 2004.

Ramsey, Paul. *Fabricated Man: The Ethics of Genetic Control*. New Haven, CT: Yale University Press, 1970.

Randers, J., Rockström, J., Stoknes, P. E., Golüke, U., Collste, D., and Cornell, S. 2018. *Transformation Is Feasible: How to Achieve the Sustainable Development Goals within Planetary Boundaries. A report to the Club of Rome from Stockholm Resilience Centre and BI Norwegian Business School*. 2018. www.stockholmresilience.org/publications/artiklar/2018-10-17-transformation-is-feasible–how-to-achieve-the-sustainable–development-goals-within-planetary-boundaries.html.

Rendtorff, Jacob Dahl, and Kemp, Peter. *Basic Ethical Principles in European Bioethics and Biolaw* Vol. I *Autonomy, Dignity, Integrity and Vulnerability*. Copenhagen and Barcelona: Centre for Ethics and Law and Institut Borja de Bioética, 2000.

Rhodes, Rosamond. Genetic Links, Family Ties and Social Bonds: Rights and Responsibilities in the Face of Genetic Knowledge. *Journal of Medicine and Philosophy* 23 (1998): 10–30.

Rhodes, Rosamond, Battin, Margaret P., and Silvers, Anita, eds. *Medicine and Social Justice: Essays on the Distribution of Health Care.* New York: Oxford University Press, 2002.

Riggenbach, Jeff. *Persuaded by Reason: Joan Kennedy Taylor and the Rebirth of American Individualism.* New York: Cook & Taylor, 2014.

Ritner, Susan Rennie. The Dutch Reformed Church and Apartheid. *Journal of Contemporary History* 2 (1967): 17–37. https://doi.org/10.1177/00220094 6700200404.

Ryan, John Augustine. Theories of Population. *The Catholic Encyclopedia* Vol. 12. New York: Robert Appleton Company, 1911. www.newadvent.org/cathen/12276a.htm.

Sandel, Michael. *The Case Against Perfection: Ethics in the Age of Genetic Engineering.* Cambridge, MA: The Belknap Press of Harvard University Press, 2007.

Savulescu, Julian. Procreative Beneficence: Why We Should Select the Best Children. *Bioethics* 15 (2001): 413–26.

Schendel, Gordon. *Medicine in Mexico: From Aztec Herbs to Betatrons.* Austin: University of Texas Press, 1968.

Schiermeier, Quirin. Gloomy 1970s Predictions about Earth's Fate Still Hold True. *Nature News* October 18, 2018. www.nature.com/articles/d41586-018-07117-2.

Schroeder-Lein, Glenna R., ed. *The Encyclopedia of Civil War Medicine.* London: Routledge, 2008.

Sherwin, Susan. *No Longer Patient: Feminist Ethics and Health Care.* Philadelphia, PA: Temple University Press, 1992.

Sidgwick, Henry. *The Methods of Ethics* [original 1874]. Seventh edition. Indianapolis, IN: Hackett Publishing Company, 1981.

Singer, Peter. *Democracy and Disobedience.* Oxford: Clarendon Press, 1973.

Singer, Peter. *Practical Ethics.* Cambridge: Cambridge University Press, 1979.

Singer, Peter. *Practical Ethics.* Third edition. Cambridge: Cambridge University Press, 2011.

Singer, Peter, and Cavalieri, Paola. *The Great Ape Project.* New York: St. Martin's Press, 1993.

Singer, Peter, and Wells, Deane. *The Reproduction Revolution: New Ways of Making Babies.* Oxford: Oxford University Press, 1984.

Smart, J. J. C., and Williams, Bernard. *Utilitarianism: For and Against.* Cambridge: Cambridge University Press, 1973.

Smith, Adam. *An Inquiry into the Nature and Causes of the Wealth of Nations* [original 1776]. Fifth edition. Cannan, Edwin, ed. London: Methuen and Co., 1904.

Stevis-Gridneff, Matina. E.U. Climate Plan Would Sweeten Deal for Coal Countries. *The New York Times* December 11, 2019. www.nytimes.com/2019/12/11/world/europe/eu-climate-plan-coal.html.

Takala, Tuija. *Genes, Sense and Sensibility: Philosophical Studies on the Ethics of Modern Biotechnologies*. Turku: University of Turku, 2000.

Takala, Tuija. What Is Wrong with Global Bioethics? On the Limitations of the Four Principles Approach. *Cambridge Quarterly of Healthcare Ethics* 10 (2001): 72–7.

Takala, Tuija, and Häyry, Matti. Genetic Ignorance, Moral Obligations and Social Duties. *Journal of Medicine and Philosophy* 25 (2000): 107–13.

Tangwa, Godfrey B., ed. *African Perspectives on Some Contemporary Bioethics Problems*. Newcastle upon Tyne: Cambridge Scholars Publishing, 2019.

Thomson, Judith Jarvis. A Defense of Abortion. *Philosophy & Public Affairs* 1 (1971): 47–66.

Tong, Rosemary, and Williams, Nancy. Gender Justice in the Health-Care System: Past Experiences, Present Realities, and Future Hopes. In Rosamond Rhodes, Margaret P. Battin, and Anita Silvers, eds. *Medicine and Social Justice: Essays on the Distribution of Health Care*. New York: Oxford University Press, 2002: 224–34.

United Nations. *Report of the World Commission on Environment and Development: Our Common Future*. 1987. www.are.admin.ch/are/en/home/media/publications/sustainable-development/brundtland-report.html.

United Nations. *Transforming Our World: The 2030 Agenda for Sustainable Development*. 2015. www.un.org/ga/search/view_doc.asp?symbol=A/RES/70/1&Lang=E.

Vermeulen P., and De Jongh, D. Parameter Sensitivity of the "Limits to Growth" World Model. *Applied Mathematical Modelling* 1 (1976): 29–32.

Vogt, William. *Road to Survival*. New York: W. Sloane Associates, 1948.

Warren, Mary Ann. On the Moral and Legal Status of Abortion. *The Monist* 57 (1973): 43–61.

Whelan, Daniel J. *Indivisible Human Rights: A History*. Philadelphia: University of Pennsylvania Press, 2010.

Widdows, Heather. *Global Ethics: An Introduction*. London: Routledge, 2011.

Widdows, Heather, Dickenson, Donna, and Hellsten, Sirkku. Global Bioethics. *New Review of Bioethics* 1 (2003): 101–16.

World Medical Association. *Declaration of Geneva: The "Modern Hippocratic Oath."* 1947. www.wma.net/what-we-do/medical-ethics/declaration-of-geneva/.

World Medical Association. *WMA Declaration of Geneva*. 2018. www.wma.net/policies-post/wma-declaration-of-geneva/.

Acknowledgments

My thanks are due, for financial support, to the Academy of Finland (project SA 307467 "Bioeconomy and Justice") and the Ministry of Agriculture and Forestry of Finland (projects VN/2470/2022 "Justainability," 101/03.02.06.00/2018 "The Role of Justice in Decision Making Concerning Bioeconomy," and 2142/03.02.06.00/2018 "A Just Management Model for a Systemic and Sustainable Shift Towards Bioeconomy").

Cambridge Elements

Bioethics and Neuroethics

Thomasine Kushner

California Pacific Medical Center, San Francisco

Thomasine Kushner, PhD, is the founding Editor of the *Cambridge Quarterly of Healthcare Ethics* and coordinates the International Bioethics Retreat, where bioethicists share their current research projects, the Cambridge Consortium for Bioethics Education, a growing network of global bioethics educators, and the Cambridge-ICM Neuroethics Network, which provides a setting for leading brain scientists and ethicists to learn from each other.

About the Series

Bioethics and neuroethics play pivotal roles in today's debates in philosophy, science, law, and health policy. With the rapid growth of scientific and technological advances, their importance will only increase. This series provides focused and comprehensive coverage in both disciplines consisting of foundational topics, current subjects under discussion and views toward future developments.

Cambridge Elements ≡

Bioethics and Neuroethics

Printed in the United States
by Baker & Taylor Publisher Services